C-758    CAREER EXAMINATION SERIES

*This is your*
*PASSBOOK for...*

# Stationary Engineer

*Test Preparation Study Guide*
*Questions & Answers*

NATIONAL LEARNING CORPORATION®

# COPYRIGHT NOTICE

This book is SOLELY intended for, is sold ONLY to, and its use is RESTRICTED to individual, bona fide applicants or candidates who qualify by virtue of having seriously filed applications for appropriate license, certificate, professional and/or promotional advancement, higher school matriculation, scholarship, or other legitimate requirements of education and/or governmental authorities.

This book is NOT intended for use, class instruction, tutoring, training, duplication, copying, reprinting, excerption, or adaptation, etc., by:

1) Other publishers
2) Proprietors and/or Instructors of "Coaching" and/or Preparatory Courses
3) Personnel and/or Training Divisions of commercial, industrial, and governmental organizations
4) Schools, colleges, or universities and/or their departments and staffs, including teachers and other personnel
5) Testing Agencies or Bureaus
6) Study groups which seek by the purchase of a single volume to copy and/or duplicate and/or adapt this material for use by the group as a whole without having purchased individual volumes for each of the members of the group
7) Et al.

Such persons would be in violation of appropriate Federal and State statutes.

PROVISION OF LICENSING AGREEMENTS – Recognized educational, commercial, industrial, and governmental institutions and organizations, and others legitimately engaged in educational pursuits, including training, testing, and measurement activities, may address request for a licensing agreement to the copyright owners, who will determine whether, and under what conditions, including fees and charges, the materials in this book may be used them.  In other words, a licensing facility exists for the legitimate use of the material in this book on other than an individual basis.  However, it is asseverated and affirmed here that the material in this book CANNOT be used without the receipt of the express permission of such a licensing agreement from the Publishers. Inquiries re licensing should be addressed to the company, attention rights and permissions department.

All rights reserved, including the right of reproduction in whole or in part, in any form or by any means, electronic or mechanical, including photocopying, recording, or by any information storage and retrieval system, without permission in writing from the Publisher.

Copyright © 2024 by
## National Learning Corporation

212 Michael Drive, Syosset, NY 11791
(516) 921-8888 • www.passbooks.com
E-mail: info@passbooks.com

PUBLISHED IN THE UNITED STATES OF AMERICA

# PASSBOOK® SERIES

THE *PASSBOOK® SERIES* has been created to prepare applicants and candidates for the ultimate academic battlefield – the examination room.

At some time in our lives, each and every one of us may be required to take an examination – for validation, matriculation, admission, qualification, registration, certification, or licensure.

Based on the assumption that every applicant or candidate has met the basic formal educational standards, has taken the required number of courses, and read the necessary texts, the *PASSBOOK® SERIES* furnishes the one special preparation which may assure passing with confidence, instead of failing with insecurity. Examination questions – together with answers – are furnished as the basic vehicle for study so that the mysteries of the examination and its compounding difficulties may be eliminated or diminished by a sure method.

This book is meant to help you pass your examination provided that you qualify and are serious in your objective.

The entire field is reviewed through the huge store of content information which is succinctly presented through a provocative and challenging approach – the question-and-answer method.

A climate of success is established by furnishing the correct answers at the end of each test.

You soon learn to recognize types of questions, forms of questions, and patterns of questioning. You may even begin to anticipate expected outcomes.

You perceive that many questions are repeated or adapted so that you can gain acute insights, which may enable you to score many sure points.

You learn how to confront new questions, or types of questions, and to attack them confidently and work out the correct answers.

You note objectives and emphases, and recognize pitfalls and dangers, so that you may make positive educational adjustments.

Moreover, you are kept fully informed in relation to new concepts, methods, practices, and directions in the field.

You discover that you are actually taking the examination all the time: you are preparing for the examination by "taking" an examination, not by reading extraneous and/or supererogatory textbooks.

In short, this PASSBOOK®, used directedly, should be an important factor in helping you to pass your test.

# STATIONARY ENGINEER

## DUTIES
Stationary Engineers, under supervision, operate, maintain and adjust steam power plant and electro-mechanical building equipment and supervise the daily operation and maintenance of boiler and refrigeration equipment and related heating and ventilating equipment to ensure proper room temperatures in all buildings. They operate, maintain and adjust boilers, furnaces, engines, pumps, heat exchangers, generators, motors, chillers, cooling towers, equipment for heating, ventilating, air conditioning, lighting and associated equipment in public buildings, municipal pumping stations and incinerators; make periodic inspections of equipment and minor repairs to such equipment; perform preventive maintenance; take responsible charge of a watch, and while so engaged are responsible for and direct subordinate personnel; may operate control consoles in control rooms; prepare requisitions for materials and spare parts; instruct and train subordinates and other personnel; read meters, gauges, and other recording devices and log the data; keep records and make reports; as directed, inspect low pressure boilers in accordance with a unified inspection procedure. Performs related duties as required.

## KNOWLEDGE AND ABILITIES
Knowledge of:
1. Heating, ventilation, and air conditioning (HVAC) systems, to assess repair needs and determine the proper course of action to fix malfunctioning units.
2. Elements of a refrigeration system (e.g., compressors, condensers, evaporators, traps, pumps, valves) to assess repair needs and determine the proper course of action to fix malfunctioning units.
3. Building electric and pneumatic controls to assess building functions and determine the need for repair and replacement of action to fix malfunctioning units.
4. Building electric and pneumatic controls to assess building functions and determine the need for repair and/or replacement of building systems.
5. Electrical, water sewage, and other mechanical systems to assess repair needs and determine the proper course of action to fix malfunctioning units.
6. The principles and methods (e.g., sequences of installation, coordination with other trades, conduit bending wire pulling, rating of equipment) used in the installation, maintenance, and repair of electrical systems and components (e.g., wiring, switches, lighting, transformers, high voltage, switchboards, motor control centers) to accomplish work assignments.
7. Materials, tools, and equipment (e.g., cable reels, conduit benders stripping tools, voltage or current meters, wire or cable cutters) used in the installation, maintenance, and repair of electrical systems and components (e.g., wiring, switches, lighting, transformers, high voltage, switchboard, motor control centers, control modules, control boards) to accomplish work assignments.
8. Materials, tools, and equipment (e.g., cable reels, conduit benders, stripping tools, voltage or current meters, wire or cable cutters) used in the installation, maintenance, and repair of electrical systems and components (e.g., wiring, switches, lighting, transformers, high voltage, switchboard, motor control centers, control modules, control boards) to accomplish work assignments.
9. The principles and operations of electrical equipment (e.g., wiring, switches, lighting, transformers, switchboards, motor control centers, control modules, control boards) for the installation, maintenance, alteration and repair of electrical systems and components.
10. Organizational policies and procedures to maintain safety and security of facilities/departments, staff, and property.

11. Boilers and auxiliary boiler equipment to determine proper maintenance and care of facilities.
12. Gas and water distribution systems to assess functionality of building systems and determine when repairs are needed.
13. Steam distribution systems to assess functionality of building systems and determine when repairs are needed.
14. Building water and sewage systems to assess building functions and determine the need for repair of building systems.
15. Tools used by various trades (e.g., electrician, plumber, carpenter, stationary engineer) used in the maintenance and repair of building facilities.
16. Basic mathematical operations and calculations (e.g., addition, subtraction, multiplication, division, percentages, order of operations, fractions) to calculate labor, materials, and/or cost estimates for projects and work orders.

Ability to:

17. Perform basic mathematical computations (e.g., addition, subtraction, multiplication, division, ratios, percentages) to calculate labor, materials, and/or cost estimates for projects, work orders and additions.
18. Convert between units of measurement (e.g., temperature, energy, volume, mass) to calculate workloads and complete project work.
19. Determine the accuracy of various mathematical calculations (e.g., addition, subtraction, multiplication, division, ratios, percentages) to verify labor, materials, and/or cost estimates for projects, work orders and additions.

## SCOPE OF THE EXAMINATION

The written test will cover knowledge, skills, and/or abilities in such areas as:

1. **Operation, maintenance and repair of steam-generating systems including related mechanical and electrical equipment** - These questions test for knowledge of the operating principles involved in various types of steam boilers and their accessories; the proper operating practices used when working with steam generating systems; and the functions of the various types of auxiliary mechanical and electrical equipment found in steam generating systems.
2. **Air conditioning and refrigeration systems** - These questions test for knowledge of the operating principles and practices involved in air conditioning and refrigeration systems; characteristics of various refrigerants; the refrigeration cycle; and proper maintenance and upkeep of air conditioning systems and their related components.
3. **Reading of scales and gauges** - These questions test for the ability to read and interpret information displayed on various types of scales, gauges, and meters.
4. **Operation and maintenance of heating and ventilating systems including steam distribution** -These questions test for knowledge of the operating principles and practices involved in steam heating and air handling systems including ventilation equipment, temperature controllers, and typical steam heating and heat distribution methods and equipment.
5. **Mechanical and electrical trades** - These questions test for knowledge of the principles and practices involved in installing, operating, maintaining, and repairing various types of electrical and mechanical equipment used in heating and ventilating systems.

# HOW TO TAKE A TEST

I. YOU MUST PASS AN EXAMINATION

A. *WHAT EVERY CANDIDATE SHOULD KNOW*

Examination applicants often ask us for help in preparing for the written test. What can I study in advance? What kinds of questions will be asked? How will the test be given? How will the papers be graded?

As an applicant for a civil service examination, you may be wondering about some of these things. Our purpose here is to suggest effective methods of advance study and to describe civil service examinations.

Your chances for success on this examination can be increased if you know how to prepare. Those "pre-examination jitters" can be reduced if you know what to expect. You can even experience an adventure in good citizenship if you know why civil service exams are given.

B. *WHY ARE CIVIL SERVICE EXAMINATIONS GIVEN?*

Civil service examinations are important to you in two ways. As a citizen, you want public jobs filled by employees who know how to do their work. As a job seeker, you want a fair chance to compete for that job on an equal footing with other candidates. The best-known means of accomplishing this two-fold goal is the competitive examination.

Exams are widely publicized throughout the nation. They may be administered for jobs in federal, state, city, municipal, town or village governments or agencies.

Any citizen may apply, with some limitations, such as the age or residence of applicants. Your experience and education may be reviewed to see whether you meet the requirements for the particular examination. When these requirements exist, they are reasonable and applied consistently to all applicants. Thus, a competitive examination may cause you some uneasiness now, but it is your privilege and safeguard.

C. *HOW ARE CIVIL SERVICE EXAMS DEVELOPED?*

Examinations are carefully written by trained technicians who are specialists in the field known as "psychological measurement," in consultation with recognized authorities in the field of work that the test will cover. These experts recommend the subject matter areas or skills to be tested; only those knowledges or skills important to your success on the job are included. The most reliable books and source materials available are used as references. Together, the experts and technicians judge the difficulty level of the questions.

Test technicians know how to phrase questions so that the problem is clearly stated. Their ethics do not permit "trick" or "catch" questions. Questions may have been tried out on sample groups, or subjected to statistical analysis, to determine their usefulness.

Written tests are often used in combination with performance tests, ratings of training and experience, and oral interviews. All of these measures combine to form the best-known means of finding the right person for the right job.

## II. HOW TO PASS THE WRITTEN TEST

### A. NATURE OF THE EXAMINATION

To prepare intelligently for civil service examinations, you should know how they differ from school examinations you have taken. In school you were assigned certain definite pages to read or subjects to cover. The examination questions were quite detailed and usually emphasized memory. Civil service exams, on the other hand, try to discover your present ability to perform the duties of a position, plus your potentiality to learn these duties. In other words, a civil service exam attempts to predict how successful you will be. Questions cover such a broad area that they cannot be as minute and detailed as school exam questions.

In the public service similar kinds of work, or positions, are grouped together in one "class." This process is known as *position-classification*. All the positions in a class are paid according to the salary range for that class. One class title covers all of these positions, and they are all tested by the same examination.

### B. FOUR BASIC STEPS

#### 1) Study the announcement

How, then, can you know what subjects to study? Our best answer is: "Learn as much as possible about the class of positions for which you've applied." The exam will test the knowledge, skills and abilities needed to do the work.

Your most valuable source of information about the position you want is the official exam announcement. This announcement lists the training and experience qualifications. Check these standards and apply only if you come reasonably close to meeting them.

The brief description of the position in the examination announcement offers some clues to the subjects which will be tested. Think about the job itself. Review the duties in your mind. Can you perform them, or are there some in which you are rusty? Fill in the blank spots in your preparation.

Many jurisdictions preview the written test in the exam announcement by including a section called "Knowledge and Abilities Required," "Scope of the Examination," or some similar heading. Here you will find out specifically what fields will be tested.

#### 2) Review your own background

Once you learn in general what the position is all about, and what you need to know to do the work, ask yourself which subjects you already know fairly well and which need improvement. You may wonder whether to concentrate on improving your strong areas or on building some background in your fields of weakness. When the announcement has specified "some knowledge" or "considerable knowledge," or has used adjectives like "beginning principles of…" or "advanced … methods," you can get a clue as to the number and difficulty of questions to be asked in any given field. More questions, and hence broader coverage, would be included for those subjects which are more important in the work. Now weigh your strengths and weaknesses against the job requirements and prepare accordingly.

#### 3) Determine the level of the position

Another way to tell how intensively you should prepare is to understand the level of the job for which you are applying. Is it the entering level? In other words, is this the position in which beginners in a field of work are hired? Or is it an intermediate or advanced level? Sometimes this is indicated by such words as "Junior" or "Senior" in the class title. Other jurisdictions use Roman numerals to designate the level – Clerk I, Clerk II, for example. The word "Supervisor" sometimes appears in the title. If the level is not indicated by the title, check the description of duties. Will you be working under very close supervision, or will you have responsibility for independent decisions in this work?

**4) Choose appropriate study materials**

Now that you know the subjects to be examined and the relative amount of each subject to be covered, you can choose suitable study materials. For beginning level jobs, or even advanced ones, if you have a pronounced weakness in some aspect of your training, read a modern, standard textbook in that field. Be sure it is up to date and has general coverage. Such books are normally available at your library, and the librarian will be glad to help you locate one. For entry-level positions, questions of appropriate difficulty are chosen -- neither highly advanced questions, nor those too simple. Such questions require careful thought but not advanced training.

If the position for which you are applying is technical or advanced, you will read more advanced, specialized material. If you are already familiar with the basic principles of your field, elementary textbooks would waste your time. Concentrate on advanced textbooks and technical periodicals. Think through the concepts and review difficult problems in your field.

These are all general sources. You can get more ideas on your own initiative, following these leads. For example, training manuals and publications of the government agency which employs workers in your field can be useful, particularly for technical and professional positions. A letter or visit to the government department involved may result in more specific study suggestions, and certainly will provide you with a more definite idea of the exact nature of the position you are seeking.


## III. KINDS OF TESTS

Tests are used for purposes other than measuring knowledge and ability to perform specified duties. For some positions, it is equally important to test ability to make adjustments to new situations or to profit from training. In others, basic mental abilities not dependent on information are essential. Questions which test these things may not appear as pertinent to the duties of the position as those which test for knowledge and information. Yet they are often highly important parts of a fair examination. For very general questions, it is almost impossible to help you direct your study efforts. What we can do is to point out some of the more common of these general abilities needed in public service positions and describe some typical questions.

1) General information

Broad, general information has been found useful for predicting job success in some kinds of work. This is tested in a variety of ways, from vocabulary lists to questions about current events. Basic background in some field of work, such as sociology or economics, may be sampled in a group of questions. Often these are principles which have become familiar to most persons through exposure rather than through formal training. It is difficult to advise you how to study for these questions; being alert to the world around you is our best suggestion.

2) Verbal ability

An example of an ability needed in many positions is verbal or language ability. Verbal ability is, in brief, the ability to use and understand words. Vocabulary and grammar tests are typical measures of this ability. Reading comprehension or paragraph interpretation questions are common in many kinds of civil service tests. You are given a paragraph of written material and asked to find its central meaning.

3) Numerical ability

Number skills can be tested by the familiar arithmetic problem, by checking paired lists of numbers to see which are alike and which are different, or by interpreting charts and graphs. In the latter test, a graph may be printed in the test booklet which you are asked to use as the basis for answering questions.

4) Observation

A popular test for law-enforcement positions is the observation test. A picture is shown to you for several minutes, then taken away. Questions about the picture test your ability to observe both details and larger elements.

5) Following directions

In many positions in the public service, the employee must be able to carry out written instructions dependably and accurately. You may be given a chart with several columns, each column listing a variety of information. The questions require you to carry out directions involving the information given in the chart.

6) Skills and aptitudes

Performance tests effectively measure some manual skills and aptitudes. When the skill is one in which you are trained, such as typing or shorthand, you can practice. These tests are often very much like those given in business school or high school courses. For many of the other skills and aptitudes, however, no short-time preparation can be made. Skills and abilities natural to you or that you have developed throughout your lifetime are being tested.

Many of the general questions just described provide all the data needed to answer the questions and ask you to use your reasoning ability to find the answers. Your best preparation for these tests, as well as for tests of facts and ideas, is to be at your physical and mental best. You, no doubt, have your own methods of getting into an exam-taking mood and keeping "in shape." The next section lists some ideas on this subject.


IV. KINDS OF QUESTIONS

Only rarely is the "essay" question, which you answer in narrative form, used in civil service tests. Civil service tests are usually of the short-answer type. Full instructions for answering these questions will be given to you at the examination. But in case this is your first experience with short-answer questions and separate answer sheets, here is what you need to know:

**1) Multiple-choice Questions**

Most popular of the short-answer questions is the "multiple choice" or "best answer" question. It can be used, for example, to test for factual knowledge, ability to solve problems or judgment in meeting situations found at work.

A multiple-choice question is normally one of three types—
- It can begin with an incomplete statement followed by several possible endings. You are to find the one ending which *best* completes the statement, although some of the others may not be entirely wrong.
- It can also be a complete statement in the form of a question which is answered by choosing one of the statements listed.

- It can be in the form of a problem – again you select the best answer.

Here is an example of a multiple-choice question with a discussion which should give you some clues as to the method for choosing the right answer:

When an employee has a complaint about his assignment, the action which will *best* help him overcome his difficulty is to
   A. discuss his difficulty with his coworkers
   B. take the problem to the head of the organization
   C. take the problem to the person who gave him the assignment
   D. say nothing to anyone about his complaint

In answering this question, you should study each of the choices to find which is best. Consider choice "A" – Certainly an employee may discuss his complaint with fellow employees, but no change or improvement can result, and the complaint remains unresolved. Choice "B" is a poor choice since the head of the organization probably does not know what assignment you have been given, and taking your problem to him is known as "going over the head" of the supervisor. The supervisor, or person who made the assignment, is the person who can clarify it or correct any injustice. Choice "C" is, therefore, correct. To say nothing, as in choice "D," is unwise. Supervisors have and interest in knowing the problems employees are facing, and the employee is seeking a solution to his problem.

## 2) True/False Questions

The "true/false" or "right/wrong" form of question is sometimes used. Here a complete statement is given. Your job is to decide whether the statement is right or wrong.

SAMPLE: A roaming cell-phone call to a nearby city costs less than a non-roaming call to a distant city.

This statement is wrong, or false, since roaming calls are more expensive.

This is not a complete list of all possible question forms, although most of the others are variations of these common types. You will always get complete directions for answering questions. Be sure you understand *how* to mark your answers – ask questions until you do.

## V. RECORDING YOUR ANSWERS

Computer terminals are used more and more today for many different kinds of exams.

For an examination with very few applicants, you may be told to record your answers in the test booklet itself. Separate answer sheets are much more common. If this separate answer sheet is to be scored by machine – and this is often the case – it is highly important that you mark your answers correctly in order to get credit.

An electronic scoring machine is often used in civil service offices because of the speed with which papers can be scored. Machine-scored answer sheets must be marked with a pencil, which will be given to you. This pencil has a high graphite content which responds to the electronic scoring machine. As a matter of fact, stray dots may register as answers, so do not let your pencil rest on the answer sheet while you are pondering the correct answer. Also, if your pencil lead breaks or is otherwise defective, ask for another.

Since the answer sheet will be dropped in a slot in the scoring machine, be careful not to bend the corners or get the paper crumpled.

The answer sheet normally has five vertical columns of numbers, with 30 numbers to a column. These numbers correspond to the question numbers in your test booklet. After each number, going across the page are four or five pairs of dotted lines. These short dotted lines have small letters or numbers above them. The first two pairs may also have a "T" or "F" above the letters. This indicates that the first two pairs only are to be used if the questions are of the true-false type. If the questions are multiple choice, disregard the "T" and "F" and pay attention only to the small letters or numbers.

Answer your questions in the manner of the sample that follows:

32. The largest city in the United States is
    A. Washington, D.C.
    B. New York City
    C. Chicago
    D. Detroit
    E. San Francisco

1) Choose the answer you think is best. (New York City is the largest, so "B" is correct.)
2) Find the row of dotted lines numbered the same as the question you are answering. (Find row number 32)
3) Find the pair of dotted lines corresponding to the answer. (Find the pair of lines under the mark "B.")
4) Make a solid black mark between the dotted lines.


## VI. BEFORE THE TEST

Common sense will help you find procedures to follow to get ready for an examination. Too many of us, however, overlook these sensible measures. Indeed, nervousness and fatigue have been found to be the most serious reasons why applicants fail to do their best on civil service tests. Here is a list of reminders:

- Begin your preparation early – Don't wait until the last minute to go scurrying around for books and materials or to find out what the position is all about.
- Prepare continuously – An hour a night for a week is better than an all-night cram session. This has been definitely established. What is more, a night a week for a month will return better dividends than crowding your study into a shorter period of time.
- Locate the place of the exam – You have been sent a notice telling you when and where to report for the examination. If the location is in a different town or otherwise unfamiliar to you, it would be well to inquire the best route and learn something about the building.
- Relax the night before the test – Allow your mind to rest. Do not study at all that night. Plan some mild recreation or diversion; then go to bed early and get a good night's sleep.
- Get up early enough to make a leisurely trip to the place for the test – This way unforeseen events, traffic snarls, unfamiliar buildings, etc. will not upset you.
- Dress comfortably – A written test is not a fashion show. You will be known by number and not by name, so wear something comfortable.

- Leave excess paraphernalia at home – Shopping bags and odd bundles will get in your way. You need bring only the items mentioned in the official notice you received; usually everything you need is provided. Do not bring reference books to the exam. They will only confuse those last minutes and be taken away from you when in the test room.
- Arrive somewhat ahead of time – If because of transportation schedules you must get there very early, bring a newspaper or magazine to take your mind off yourself while waiting.
- Locate the examination room – When you have found the proper room, you will be directed to the seat or part of the room where you will sit. Sometimes you are given a sheet of instructions to read while you are waiting. Do not fill out any forms until you are told to do so; just read them and be prepared.
- Relax and prepare to listen to the instructions
- If you have any physical problem that may keep you from doing your best, be sure to tell the test administrator. If you are sick or in poor health, you really cannot do your best on the exam. You can come back and take the test some other time.

## VII. AT THE TEST

The day of the test is here and you have the test booklet in your hand. The temptation to get going is very strong. Caution! There is more to success than knowing the right answers. You must know how to identify your papers and understand variations in the type of short-answer question used in this particular examination. Follow these suggestions for maximum results from your efforts:

### 1) Cooperate with the monitor
The test administrator has a duty to create a situation in which you can be as much at ease as possible. He will give instructions, tell you when to begin, check to see that you are marking your answer sheet correctly, and so on. He is not there to guard you, although he will see that your competitors do not take unfair advantage. He wants to help you do your best.

### 2) Listen to all instructions
Don't jump the gun! Wait until you understand all directions. In most civil service tests you get more time than you need to answer the questions. So don't be in a hurry. Read each word of instructions until you clearly understand the meaning. Study the examples, listen to all announcements and follow directions. Ask questions if you do not understand what to do.

### 3) Identify your papers
Civil service exams are usually identified by number only. You will be assigned a number; you must not put your name on your test papers. Be sure to copy your number correctly. Since more than one exam may be given, copy your exact examination title.

### 4) Plan your time
Unless you are told that a test is a "speed" or "rate of work" test, speed itself is usually not important. Time enough to answer all the questions will be provided, but this does not mean that you have all day. An overall time limit has been set. Divide the total time (in minutes) by the number of questions to determine the approximate time you have for each question.

### 5) Do not linger over difficult questions

If you come across a difficult question, mark it with a paper clip (useful to have along) and come back to it when you have been through the booklet. One caution if you do this – be sure to skip a number on your answer sheet as well. Check often to be sure that you have not lost your place and that you are marking in the row numbered the same as the question you are answering.

### 6) Read the questions

Be sure you know what the question asks! Many capable people are unsuccessful because they failed to *read* the questions correctly.

### 7) Answer all questions

Unless you have been instructed that a penalty will be deducted for incorrect answers, it is better to guess than to omit a question.

### 8) Speed tests

It is often better NOT to guess on speed tests. It has been found that on timed tests people are tempted to spend the last few seconds before time is called in marking answers at random – without even reading them – in the hope of picking up a few extra points. To discourage this practice, the instructions may warn you that your score will be "corrected" for guessing. That is, a penalty will be applied. The incorrect answers will be deducted from the correct ones, or some other penalty formula will be used.

### 9) Review your answers

If you finish before time is called, go back to the questions you guessed or omitted to give them further thought. Review other answers if you have time.

### 10) Return your test materials

If you are ready to leave before others have finished or time is called, take ALL your materials to the monitor and leave quietly. Never take any test material with you. The monitor can discover whose papers are not complete, and taking a test booklet may be grounds for disqualification.

## VIII. EXAMINATION TECHNIQUES

1) Read the general instructions carefully. These are usually printed on the first page of the exam booklet. As a rule, these instructions refer to the timing of the examination; the fact that you should not start work until the signal and must stop work at a signal, etc. If there are any *special* instructions, such as a choice of questions to be answered, make sure that you note this instruction carefully.

2) When you are ready to start work on the examination, that is as soon as the signal has been given, read the instructions to each question booklet, underline any key words or phrases, such as *least, best, outline, describe* and the like. In this way you will tend to answer as requested rather than discover on reviewing your paper that you *listed without describing*, that you selected the *worst* choice rather than the *best* choice, etc.

3) If the examination is of the objective or multiple-choice type – that is, each question will also give a series of possible answers: A, B, C or D, and you are called upon to select the best answer and write the letter next to that answer on your answer paper – it is advisable to start answering each question in turn. There may be anywhere from 50 to 100 such questions in the three or four hours allotted and you can see how much time would be taken if you read through all the questions before beginning to answer any. Furthermore, if you come across a question or group of questions which you know would be difficult to answer, it would undoubtedly affect your handling of all the other questions.

4) If the examination is of the essay type and contains but a few questions, it is a moot point as to whether you should read all the questions before starting to answer any one. Of course, if you are given a choice – say five out of seven and the like – then it is essential to read all the questions so you can eliminate the two that are most difficult. If, however, you are asked to answer all the questions, there may be danger in trying to answer the easiest one first because you may find that you will spend too much time on it. The best technique is to answer the first question, then proceed to the second, etc.

5) Time your answers. Before the exam begins, write down the time it started, then add the time allowed for the examination and write down the time it must be completed, then divide the time available somewhat as follows:
    - If 3-1/2 hours are allowed, that would be 210 minutes. If you have 80 objective-type questions, that would be an average of 2-1/2 minutes per question. Allow yourself no more than 2 minutes per question, or a total of 160 minutes, which will permit about 50 minutes to review.
    - If for the time allotment of 210 minutes there are 7 essay questions to answer, that would average about 30 minutes a question. Give yourself only 25 minutes per question so that you have about 35 minutes to review.

6) The most important instruction is to *read each question* and make sure you know what is wanted. The second most important instruction is to *time yourself properly* so that you answer every question. The third most important instruction is to *answer every question*. Guess if you have to but include something for each question. Remember that you will receive no credit for a blank and will probably receive some credit if you write something in answer to an essay question. If you guess a letter – say "B" for a multiple-choice question – you may have guessed right. If you leave a blank as an answer to a multiple-choice question, the examiners may respect your feelings but it will not add a point to your score. Some exams may penalize you for wrong answers, so in such cases *only*, you may not want to guess unless you have some basis for your answer.

7) Suggestions
    a. Objective-type questions
        1. Examine the question booklet for proper sequence of pages and questions
        2. Read all instructions carefully
        3. Skip any question which seems too difficult; return to it after all other questions have been answered
        4. Apportion your time properly; do not spend too much time on any single question or group of questions

5. Note and underline key words – *all, most, fewest, least, best, worst, same, opposite*, etc.
6. Pay particular attention to negatives
7. Note unusual option, e.g., unduly long, short, complex, different or similar in content to the body of the question
8. Observe the use of "hedging" words – *probably, may, most likely*, etc.
9. Make sure that your answer is put next to the same number as the question
10. Do not second-guess unless you have good reason to believe the second answer is definitely more correct
11. Cross out original answer if you decide another answer is more accurate; do not erase until you are ready to hand your paper in
12. Answer all questions; guess unless instructed otherwise
13. Leave time for review

b. Essay questions
1. Read each question carefully
2. Determine exactly what is wanted. Underline key words or phrases.
3. Decide on outline or paragraph answer
4. Include many different points and elements unless asked to develop any one or two points or elements
5. Show impartiality by giving pros and cons unless directed to select one side only
6. Make and write down any assumptions you find necessary to answer the questions
7. Watch your English, grammar, punctuation and choice of words
8. Time your answers; don't crowd material

8) Answering the essay question

Most essay questions can be answered by framing the specific response around several key words or ideas. Here are a few such key words or ideas:

M's: manpower, materials, methods, money, management
P's: purpose, program, policy, plan, procedure, practice, problems, pitfalls, personnel, public relations

a. Six basic steps in handling problems:
1. Preliminary plan and background development
2. Collect information, data and facts
3. Analyze and interpret information, data and facts
4. Analyze and develop solutions as well as make recommendations
5. Prepare report and sell recommendations
6. Install recommendations and follow up effectiveness

b. Pitfalls to avoid
1. *Taking things for granted* – A statement of the situation does not necessarily imply that each of the elements is necessarily true; for example, a complaint may be invalid and biased so that all that can be taken for granted is that a complaint has been registered

2. *Considering only one side of a situation* – Wherever possible, indicate several alternatives and then point out the reasons you selected the best one
3. *Failing to indicate follow up* – Whenever your answer indicates action on your part, make certain that you will take proper follow-up action to see how successful your recommendations, procedures or actions turn out to be
4. *Taking too long in answering any single question* – Remember to time your answers properly

## IX. AFTER THE TEST

Scoring procedures differ in detail among civil service jurisdictions although the general principles are the same. Whether the papers are hand-scored or graded by machine we have described, they are nearly always graded by number. That is, the person who marks the paper knows only the number – never the name – of the applicant. Not until all the papers have been graded will they be matched with names. If other tests, such as training and experience or oral interview ratings have been given, scores will be combined. Different parts of the examination usually have different weights. For example, the written test might count 60 percent of the final grade, and a rating of training and experience 40 percent. In many jurisdictions, veterans will have a certain number of points added to their grades.

After the final grade has been determined, the names are placed in grade order and an eligible list is established. There are various methods for resolving ties between those who get the same final grade – probably the most common is to place first the name of the person whose application was received first. Job offers are made from the eligible list in the order the names appear on it. You will be notified of your grade and your rank as soon as all these computations have been made. This will be done as rapidly as possible.

People who are found to meet the requirements in the announcement are called "eligibles." Their names are put on a list of eligible candidates. An eligible's chances of getting a job depend on how high he stands on this list and how fast agencies are filling jobs from the list.

When a job is to be filled from a list of eligibles, the agency asks for the names of people on the list of eligibles for that job. When the civil service commission receives this request, it sends to the agency the names of the three people highest on this list. Or, if the job to be filled has specialized requirements, the office sends the agency the names of the top three persons who meet these requirements from the general list.

The appointing officer makes a choice from among the three people whose names were sent to him. If the selected person accepts the appointment, the names of the others are put back on the list to be considered for future openings.

That is the rule in hiring from all kinds of eligible lists, whether they are for typist, carpenter, chemist, or something else. For every vacancy, the appointing officer has his choice of any one of the top three eligibles on the list. This explains why the person whose name is on top of the list sometimes does not get an appointment when some of the persons lower on the list do. If the appointing officer chooses the second or third eligible, the No. 1 eligible does not get a job at once, but stays on the list until he is appointed or the list is terminated.

# X. HOW TO PASS THE INTERVIEW TEST

The examination for which you applied requires an oral interview test. You have already taken the written test and you are now being called for the interview test – the final part of the formal examination.

You may think that it is not possible to prepare for an interview test and that there are no procedures to follow during an interview. Our purpose is to point out some things you can do in advance that will help you and some good rules to follow and pitfalls to avoid while you are being interviewed.

*What is an interview supposed to test?*

The written examination is designed to test the technical knowledge and competence of the candidate; the oral is designed to evaluate intangible qualities, not readily measured otherwise, and to establish a list showing the relative fitness of each candidate – as measured against his competitors – for the position sought. Scoring is not on the basis of "right" and "wrong," but on a sliding scale of values ranging from "not passable" to "outstanding." As a matter of fact, it is possible to achieve a relatively low score without a single "incorrect" answer because of evident weakness in the qualities being measured.

Occasionally, an examination may consist entirely of an oral test – either an individual or a group oral. In such cases, information is sought concerning the technical knowledges and abilities of the candidate, since there has been no written examination for this purpose. More commonly, however, an oral test is used to supplement a written examination.

*Who conducts interviews?*

The composition of oral boards varies among different jurisdictions. In nearly all, a representative of the personnel department serves as chairman. One of the members of the board may be a representative of the department in which the candidate would work. In some cases, "outside experts" are used, and, frequently, a businessman or some other representative of the general public is asked to serve. Labor and management or other special groups may be represented. The aim is to secure the services of experts in the appropriate field.

However the board is composed, it is a good idea (and not at all improper or unethical) to ascertain in advance of the interview who the members are and what groups they represent. When you are introduced to them, you will have some idea of their backgrounds and interests, and at least you will not stutter and stammer over their names.

*What should be done before the interview?*

While knowledge about the board members is useful and takes some of the surprise element out of the interview, there is other preparation which is more substantive. It *is* possible to prepare for an oral interview – in several ways:

**1) Keep a copy of your application and review it carefully before the interview**

This may be the only document before the oral board, and the starting point of the interview. Know what education and experience you have listed there, and the sequence and dates of all of it. Sometimes the board will ask you to review the highlights of your experience for them; you should not have to hem and haw doing it.

**2) Study the class specification and the examination announcement**

Usually, the oral board has one or both of these to guide them. The qualities, characteristics or knowledges required by the position sought are stated in these documents. They offer valuable clues as to the nature of the oral interview. For example, if the job involves supervisory responsibilities, the announcement will usually indicate that knowledge of modern supervisory methods and the qualifications of the candidate as a supervisor will be tested. If so, you can expect such questions, frequently in the form of a hypothetical situation which you are expected to solve. NEVER go into an oral without knowledge of the duties and responsibilities of the job you seek.

### 3) Think through each qualification required

Try to visualize the kind of questions you would ask if you were a board member. How well could you answer them? Try especially to appraise your own knowledge and background in each area, *measured against the job sought*, and identify any areas in which you are weak. Be critical and realistic – do not flatter yourself.

### 4) Do some general reading in areas in which you feel you may be weak

For example, if the job involves supervision and your past experience has NOT, some general reading in supervisory methods and practices, particularly in the field of human relations, might be useful. Do NOT study agency procedures or detailed manuals. The oral board will be testing your understanding and capacity, not your memory.

### 5) Get a good night's sleep and watch your general health and mental attitude

You will want a clear head at the interview. Take care of a cold or any other minor ailment, and of course, no hangovers.

*What should be done on the day of the interview?*

Now comes the day of the interview itself. Give yourself plenty of time to get there. Plan to arrive somewhat ahead of the scheduled time, particularly if your appointment is in the fore part of the day. If a previous candidate fails to appear, the board might be ready for you a bit early. By early afternoon an oral board is almost invariably behind schedule if there are many candidates, and you may have to wait. Take along a book or magazine to read, or your application to review, but leave any extraneous material in the waiting room when you go in for your interview. In any event, relax and compose yourself.

The matter of dress is important. The board is forming impressions about you – from your experience, your manners, your attitude, and your appearance. Give your personal appearance careful attention. Dress your best, but not your flashiest. Choose conservative, appropriate clothing, and be sure it is immaculate. This is a business interview, and your appearance should indicate that you regard it as such. Besides, being well groomed and properly dressed will help boost your confidence.

Sooner or later, someone will call your name and escort you into the interview room. *This is it.* From here on you are on your own. It is too late for any more preparation. But remember, you asked for this opportunity to prove your fitness, and you are here because your request was granted.

*What happens when you go in?*

The usual sequence of events will be as follows: The clerk (who is often the board stenographer) will introduce you to the chairman of the oral board, who will introduce you to the other members of the board. Acknowledge the introductions before you sit down. Do not be surprised if you find a microphone facing you or a stenotypist sitting by. Oral interviews are usually recorded in the event of an appeal or other review.

Usually the chairman of the board will open the interview by reviewing the highlights of your education and work experience from your application – primarily for the benefit of the other members of the board, as well as to get the material into the record. Do not interrupt or comment unless there is an error or significant misinterpretation; if that is the case, do not hesitate. But do not quibble about insignificant matters. Also, he will usually ask you some question about your education, experience or your present job – partly to get you to start talking and to establish the interviewing "rapport." He may start the actual questioning, or turn it over to one of the other members. Frequently, each member undertakes the questioning on a particular area, one in which he is perhaps most competent, so you can expect each member to participate in the examination. Because time is limited, you may also expect some rather abrupt switches in the direction the questioning takes, so do not be upset by it. Normally, a board member will not pursue a single line of questioning unless he discovers a particular strength or weakness.

After each member has participated, the chairman will usually ask whether any member has any further questions, then will ask you if you have anything you wish to add. Unless you are expecting this question, it may floor you. Worse, it may start you off on an extended, extemporaneous speech. The board is not usually seeking more information. The question is principally to offer you a last opportunity to present further qualifications or to indicate that you have nothing to add. So, if you feel that a significant qualification or characteristic has been overlooked, it is proper to point it out in a sentence or so. Do not compliment the board on the thoroughness of their examination – they have been sketchy, and you know it. If you wish, merely say, "No thank you, I have nothing further to add." This is a point where you can "talk yourself out" of a good impression or fail to present an important bit of information. Remember, *you close the interview yourself.*

The chairman will then say, "That is all, Mr. _____, thank you." Do not be startled; the interview is over, and quicker than you think. Thank him, gather your belongings and take your leave. Save your sigh of relief for the other side of the door.

*How to put your best foot forward*

Throughout this entire process, you may feel that the board individually and collectively is trying to pierce your defenses, seek out your hidden weaknesses and embarrass and confuse you. Actually, this is not true. They are obliged to make an appraisal of your qualifications for the job you are seeking, and they want to see you in your best light. Remember, they must interview all candidates and a non-cooperative candidate may become a failure in spite of their best efforts to bring out his qualifications. Here are 15 suggestions that will help you:

**1) Be natural – Keep your attitude confident, not cocky**

If you are not confident that you can do the job, do not expect the board to be. Do not apologize for your weaknesses, try to bring out your strong points. The board is interested in a positive, not negative, presentation. Cockiness will antagonize any board member and make him wonder if you are covering up a weakness by a false show of strength.

**2) Get comfortable, but don't lounge or sprawl**

Sit erectly but not stiffly. A careless posture may lead the board to conclude that you are careless in other things, or at least that you are not impressed by the importance of the occasion. Either conclusion is natural, even if incorrect. Do not fuss with your clothing, a pencil or an ashtray. Your hands may occasionally be useful to emphasize a point; do not let them become a point of distraction.

**3) Do not wisecrack or make small talk**

This is a serious situation, and your attitude should show that you consider it as such. Further, the time of the board is limited – they do not want to waste it, and neither should you.

### 4) Do not exaggerate your experience or abilities

In the first place, from information in the application or other interviews and sources, the board may know more about you than you think. Secondly, you probably will not get away with it. An experienced board is rather adept at spotting such a situation, so do not take the chance.

### 5) If you know a board member, do not make a point of it, yet do not hide it

Certainly you are not fooling him, and probably not the other members of the board. Do not try to take advantage of your acquaintanceship – it will probably do you little good.

### 6) Do not dominate the interview

Let the board do that. They will give you the clues – do not assume that you have to do all the talking. Realize that the board has a number of questions to ask you, and do not try to take up all the interview time by showing off your extensive knowledge of the answer to the first one.

### 7) Be attentive

You only have 20 minutes or so, and you should keep your attention at its sharpest throughout. When a member is addressing a problem or question to you, give him your undivided attention. Address your reply principally to him, but do not exclude the other board members.

### 8) Do not interrupt

A board member may be stating a problem for you to analyze. He will ask you a question when the time comes. Let him state the problem, and wait for the question.

### 9) Make sure you understand the question

Do not try to answer until you are sure what the question is. If it is not clear, restate it in your own words or ask the board member to clarify it for you. However, do not haggle about minor elements.

### 10) Reply promptly but not hastily

A common entry on oral board rating sheets is "candidate responded readily," or "candidate hesitated in replies." Respond as promptly and quickly as you can, but do not jump to a hasty, ill-considered answer.

### 11) Do not be peremptory in your answers

A brief answer is proper – but do not fire your answer back. That is a losing game from your point of view. The board member can probably ask questions much faster than you can answer them.

### 12) Do not try to create the answer you think the board member wants

He is interested in what kind of mind you have and how it works – not in playing games. Furthermore, he can usually spot this practice and will actually grade you down on it.

### 13) Do not switch sides in your reply merely to agree with a board member

Frequently, a member will take a contrary position merely to draw you out and to see if you are willing and able to defend your point of view. Do not start a debate, yet do not surrender a good position. If a position is worth taking, it is worth defending.

### 14) Do not be afraid to admit an error in judgment if you are shown to be wrong

The board knows that you are forced to reply without any opportunity for careful consideration. Your answer may be demonstrably wrong. If so, admit it and get on with the interview.

### 15) Do not dwell at length on your present job

The opening question may relate to your present assignment. Answer the question but do not go into an extended discussion. You are being examined for a *new* job, not your present one. As a matter of fact, try to phrase ALL your answers in terms of the job for which you are being examined.

*Basis of Rating*

Probably you will forget most of these "do's" and "don'ts" when you walk into the oral interview room. Even remembering them all will not ensure you a passing grade. Perhaps you did not have the qualifications in the first place. But remembering them will help you to put your best foot forward, without treading on the toes of the board members.

Rumor and popular opinion to the contrary notwithstanding, an oral board wants you to make the best appearance possible. They know you are under pressure – but they also want to see how you respond to it as a guide to what your reaction would be under the pressures of the job you seek. They will be influenced by the degree of poise you display, the personal traits you show and the manner in which you respond.

## ABOUT THIS BOOK

This book contains tests divided into Examination Sections. Go through each test, answering every question in the margin. We have also attached a sample answer sheet at the back of the book that can be removed and used. At the end of each test look at the answer key and check your answers. On the ones you got wrong, look at the right answer choice and learn. Do not fill in the answers first. Do not memorize the questions and answers, but understand the answer and principles involved. On your test, the questions will likely be different from the samples. Questions are changed and new ones added. If you understand these past questions you should have success with any changes that arise. Tests may consist of several types of questions. We have additional books on each subject should more study be advisable or necessary for you. Finally, the more you study, the better prepared you will be. This book is intended to be the last thing you study before you walk into the examination room. Prior study of relevant texts is also recommended. NLC publishes some of these in our Fundamental Series. Knowledge and good sense are important factors in passing your exam. Good luck also helps. So now study this Passbook, absorb the material contained within and take that knowledge into the examination. Then do your best to pass that exam.

# EXAMINATION SECTION

# EXAMINATION SECTION
# TEST 1

DIRECTIONS: Each question or incomplete statement is followed by several suggested answers or completions. Select the one that BEST answers the question or completes the statement. *PRINT THE LETTER OF THE CORRECT ANSWER IN THE SPACE AT THE RIGHT.*

1. The one of the following gases which will NOT be found in the flue gases produced by the complete combustion of fuel oil is

    A. oxygen
    B. hydrogen
    C. nitrogen
    D. carbon dioxide

2. The amount of $CO_2$ in a flue gas sample is USUALLY stated in

    A. parts per million
    B. pounds
    C. percent
    D. pounds per mol

3. A change in the efficiency of combustion in a boiler can USUALLY be determined by comparing the previously recorded readings with the current readings of the

    A. stack temperature and $CO_2$
    B. Ringelman chart and $CO_2$
    C. stack temperature and CO
    D. over-the-fire draft and CO

4. The tube-metal temperature is appreciably higher in a superheater tube than in a boiler tube when they are both subjected to the same temperatures because the superheater tube

    A. outside gas film conductivity is higher than that of the boiler tube
    B. outside gas film conductivity is lower than that of the boiler tube
    C. inside vapor film conductivity is lower than the water film conductivity in the boiler tube
    D. inside vapor film conductivity is higher than the water film conductivity in the boiler tube

5. In a balanced draft furnace, the

    A. draft changes from positive to negative in the furnace
    B. breeching contains a barometric damper
    C. draft reading is negative at the furnace inlet
    D. draft reading is positive at the furnace outlet

6. The heating of a #6 fuel oil in an oil burner to a temperature higher than necessary solely for proper atomization is

    A. *desirable* because it can increase the burner capacity by increasing the specific volume of the oil
    B. *desirable* because it can increase the flame stability when vaporization occurs intermittently in the supply line to the burner

1

C. *undesirable* because it can decrease the burner capacity by decreasing the specific volume of the oil
D. *undesirable* because it can decrease the burner capacity by increasing the specific volume of the oil

7. In a cylindrical boiler drum, the ratio of the force tending to burst a longitudinal seam to the force tending to burst a circumferential seam is MOST NEARLY

   A. 1:1  B. 2:1  C. 3:1  D. 4:1

8. The one of the following actions an operator should NOT take to stop or decrease carry-over caused by foaming in a boiler is to

   A. lower the water level in the drum
   B. blow down the boiler
   C. increase the rate of chemical feed to the boiler
   D. reduce the steam output

9. The PRIMARY reason for treating de-aerated feedwater with sodium sulphite is to

   A. remove dissolved oxygen      B. control scale
   C. prevent carry-over           D. increase alkalinity

10. In accordance with recommended practice, a sample of boiler water for pH analysis should be taken

    A. immediately after chemicals are added to the feedwater
    B. just before bottom blowdown
    C. when the steaming rate is high
    D. prior to putting the boiler on the line

11. Of the following oil burner types, the one in which the return oil passes through the atomizer body is the

    A. rotary cup
    B. steam atomizing
    C. mechanical pressure atomizing
    D. air atomizing

12. One advantage that the mechanical pressure atomizing oil burner has over the steam atomizing oil burner is that, with the mechanical pressure atomizing oil burner, the

    A. required oil temperature is lower
    B. required pump pressure is lower
    C. range of capacity available is wider
    D. fuel is more accurately and uniformly metered

13. Of the following, the LEAST likely cause of faulty atomization of fuel oil in a rotary cup burner is

    A. too low an oil temperature
    B. carbon formation on the rotary cup
    C. too low an oil pressure
    D. insufficient secondary air

14. The device which senses the presence of the burner flame in a rotary cup oil burner is    14.____

    A. mercury tube            B. lead sulfide cell
    C. vaporstat               D. selenium rectifier

15. The component present, in GREATEST amount by weight, in #6 fuel oil is    15.____

    A. carbon      B. hydrogen      C. nitrogen      D. oxygen

16. The explosion hazard in an oil-fired boiler is usually GREATEST when    16.____

    A. lighting off
    B. securing the boiler
    C. firing at 75% of rated load
    D. firing at 100% of rated load

17. Of the following, the one which is the MOST complete and correct statement of the function of an F and T steam trap is that it removes    17.____

    A. only condensate from a steam line
    B. both condensate and non-condensable gases from a steam line
    C. only non-condensable gases from a steam line
    D. both sediment and rust particles from a steam line

18. Fire actuated fusible plugs on boilers should be renewed AT LEAST once every _____ months.    18.____

    A. 12      B. 18      C. 24      D. 30

19. A safety valve on a boiler must reach its full lift when the pressure is no GREATER than _____ above its set pressure.    19.____

    A. 3%      B. 5%      C. 7%      D. 8%

20. A device used to calibrate a steam pressure gauge is the _____ tester.    20.____

    A. spring-scale            B. dead-weight
    C. live-load               D. in-line

21. The one of the following statements that is NOT correct concerning feedwater injectors is that they are    21.____

    A. inefficient pumping units
    B. practical only on large boilers
    C. highly efficient thermally
    D. unreliable when subjected to varying loads and pressures

22. A steam pressure gauge is located 10 feet below the point where the connection is made to the top of a boiler water column. If the absolute pressure in the steam drum is 125 psi, the pressure at the gauge will be MOST NEARLY _____ psig.    22.____

    A. 102      B. 116      C. 119      D. 148

23. When comparing the operation and maintenance of a Stirling boiler with that of an equivalent horizontal straight tube boiler, the one of the following statements that is MOST complete and accurate is:    23.____

A. It is much harder to get to the tubes of a Stirling boiler for maintenance work than to a straight tube boiler with box headers
B. A Stirling boiler will steam at a lower rate than a straight tube boiler
C. Leaks occur more frequently in a Stirling boiler than in a straight tube boiler
D. The water and steam circulation rates are greater in a Stirling boiler than in a straight tube boiler

24. A supplier quotes a list price of $68.00 less discounts of 25 and 20 percent for a replacement part.
The actual cost of this item is MOST NEARLY

   A. $31     B. $34     C. $37     D. $41

25. The MAIN reason for maintaining an air dome in a pressurized house tank is to

   A. increase the tank pressure above the pump pressure
   B. avoid frequent start-and-stop pump operation
   C. force the water up to the top floor
   D. aerate the water

26. In a magnetic across-the-line starter for a 10 hp motor connected to a 4-wire, 3-phase circuit with grounded neutral, the MINIMUM required number of over-current devices is

   A. one, in the neutral conductor
   B. two, in any two conductors except the neutral
   C. three, in all conductors except the neutral
   D. four, in all four conductors

27. In order to select the correct heaters for the equipment described in Question 26 from the controller manufacturer's chart, the MOST important information needed is the

   A. power factor            B. line voltage
   C. full-load motor current D. motor horsepower

28. An electric motor, which is direct-connected to a centrifugal pump on an integral machined base, is to be replaced. In order to minimize the labor involved in replacing the motor, the specifications should include

   A. end bell size      B. serial number
   C. NEMA frame size   D. shaft size

29. A squirrel cage induction motor is rated at 5 hp when connected to a 220-volt, 3-phase, 60-cycle service.
If this motor is connected to a 208-volt, 3-phase, 60-cycle circuit, the horsepower rating would

   A. remain constant
   B. be increased by approximately 5%
   C. be decreased by approximately 10%
   D. be decreased by approximately 30%

30. A 20 hp, 230-volt DC motor operates at 75% efficiency. The full-load current, in amperes, is MOST NEARLY

   A. 45     B. 65     C. 85     D. 115

31. In a cooling tower, the water is cooled MAINLY by

   A. condensation
   B. conduction
   C. convection
   D. evaporation

32. An economizer is used with a steam boiler in order to raise the temperature of the

   A. boiler feedwater by utilizing some of the heat in the exit flue gases
   B. boiler feedwater by utilizing exhaust steam from the turbines or steam engines
   C. air used for combustion of the fuel utilizing some of the heat in the exit flue gases
   D. air used for combustion of the fuel utilizing exhaust steam from the turbines or steam engines

33. A centrifugal boiler feed pump requires 5 hp to drive it at a certain speed, total head and quantity of water delivered.
    If the speed and the quantity of water delivered are doubled and the total head quadrupled, the horsepower required will be APPROXIMATELY

   A. 10     B. 20     C. 30     D. 40

34. In a centrifugal pump installation, the available net positive suction head is NOT affected by the

   A. suction piping size and length
   B. level of the liquid supply
   C. temperature of the liquid being pumped
   D. cavitation in the pump

35. In operating a closed water circulating system, it is good practice to

   A. treat the water chemically for corrosion control
   B. drain and flush the system regularly to control corrosion
   C. leave the system undisturbed because it is sealed and needs no maintenance
   D. replace the pump shaft seals every three months

36. The function of an unloader on an electric motor-driven air compressor is to

   A. release the pressure in the cylinders in order to reduce the starting load
   B. reduce the speed of the motor when the maximum pressure is reached
   C. prevent excess pressure in the receiver
   D. drain the condensate from the cylinder head

37. The MOST highly toxic of the following refrigerants is

   A. sulphur dioxide
   B. ammonia
   C. methyl chloride
   D. freon 12

38. The MOST important objective of a safety training program should be to motivate the worker to

   A. avoid tripping hazards
   B. use hand tools properly
   C. write a clear concise accident report
   D. be constantly alert to safety hazards

39. An automatically controlled circulating water pump in a domestic hot water system is started by a device when it senses a

    A. drop in the water pressure in the circulating line
    B. drop in the water temperature in the return line
    C. rise in the water pressure in the circulating line
    D. rise in the temperature in the return line

40. In performing a hydrostatic test on an existing power boiler, the required test pressure must be controlled so that it is NOT exceeded by more than

    A. 2%   B. 4%   C. 6%   D. 8%

41. A preventive maintenance program in a boiler room should provide for routine periodic replacement of

    A. programmer electronic tubes
    B. badly leaking boiler tubes
    C. electric motors
    D. safety valve springs

42. The FIRST step to take in planning a preventive maintenance program is to

    A. replace all electric wiring
    B. make an equipment inventory
    C. replace all pump seals
    D. repair all equipment which is not in operation

43. The MOST important consideration in a fire prevention program is to

    A. train the staff to place flammables in fireproof containers
    B. know how to attack fires regardless of size
    C. see that halls, corridors, and exits are not blocked
    D. detect and eliminate every possible fire hazard

44. The type of portable fire extinguisher recommended as MOST effective for putting out oil fires is the _____ type.

    A. pump tank          B. cartridge actuated
    C. soda acid          D. foam

45. Inspecting and testing of mechanical equipment is done periodically MAINLY to

    A. help the men become more familiar with the equipment
    B. keep the men busy during slack periods
    C. encourage the men to take better care of the equipment
    D. discover minor equipment faults before they develop into major breakdowns

46. During the first stage of the high air pollution alert, plans must be made in public buildings to discontinue on-site incineration and to provide personnel and space to store the quantity of refuse that could accumulate during a period of _____ day(s).

    A. 1   B. 2   C. 5   D. 7

47. The four stages of the warning system designated by the high air pollution alert warning system are:

    A. initial, chronic, acute, penetrating
    B. forecast, alert, warning, emergency
    C. light, medium, heavy, extra heavy
    D. early, moderate, severe, toxic

48. Unless a sulphur exemption certificate is obtained, the amount of sulphur in residual fuel oil burned for heating purposes is restricted to NOT MORE than

    A. 0.2%    B. 0.3%    C. 0.55%    D. 0.7%

49. Refuse burning equipment in public buildings other than central municipal incinerators may NOT be operated except during the hours between

    A. 7 A.M. and 12 Noon         B. 7 A.M. and 5 P.M.
    C. 9 A.M. and 3 P.M.          D. 8 P.M. and 11 P.M.

50. The air contaminant detector required in a boiler installation must be adjusted to cause an audible and/or visible signal upon the emission of an air contaminant whose density, on the standard smoke chart, is GREATER than

    A. No. 1    B. No. 2    C. No. 3    D. No. 4

## KEY (CORRECT ANSWERS)

| | | | | |
|---|---|---|---|---|
| 1. B | 11. C | 21. B | 31. D | 41. A |
| 2. C | 12. D | 22. B | 32. A | 42. B |
| 3. A | 13. D | 23. D | 33. D | 43. D |
| 4. C | 14. B | 24. D | 34. D | 44. D |
| 5. A | 15. A | 25. B | 35. A | 45. D |
| 6. D | 16. A | 26. B | 36. A | 46. C |
| 7. B | 17. B | 27. C | 37. A | 47. B |
| 8. C | 18. A | 28. C | 38. D | 48. B |
| 9. A | 19. A | 29. C | 39. B | 49. B |
| 10. B | 20. B | 30. C | 40. A | 50. A |

# TEST 2

DIRECTIONS: Each question or incomplete statement is followed by several suggested answers or completions. Select the one that BEST answers the question or completes the statement. *PRINT THE LETTER OF THE CORRECT ANSWER IN THE SPACE AT THE RIGHT.*

1. The one of the following grades of fuel oil that contains the GREATEST heating value in BTU per gallon is

   A. #2  B. #4  C. #5  D. #6

   1.___

2. When we say that a fuel oil has a high viscosity, we mean MAINLY that the fuel oil will

   A. evaporate easily
   B. burn without smoke
   C. flow slowly through pipes
   D. have a low specific gravity

   2.___

3. The type of fuel oil pump GENERALLY used with a rotary cup oil burner system is the

   A. propeller pump         B. internal pump
   C. centrifugal pump       D. piston

   3.___

4. No. 6 fuel oil flowing to a mechanical atomizing burner should be preheated to APPROXIMATELY

   A. 185° F  B. 115° F  C. 100° F  D. 80° F

   4.___

5. The flame of an industrial rotary cup oil burner should be adjusted so that the flame

   A. has a yellow color with blue spots
   B. strikes all sides of the combustion chamber
   C. has a light brown color
   D. does not strike the rear of the combustion chamber

   5.___

6. The location of the oil burner *remote control switch* should GENERALLY be

   A. at the boiler room entrance
   B. on the boiler shell
   C. on the oil burner motor
   D. on a wall nearest the boiler

   6.___

7. With forced draft, the approximate wind box pressure in a single-retort underfeed stoker is NORMALLY

   A. 2"  B. 5"  C. 7"  D. 9"

   7.___

8. The pressure over the fire in a coal-fired steam boiler with a balanced-draft system and natural draft is MOST NEARLY

   A. +.60"  B. +.50"  C. -.02"  D. -.70"

   8.___

9. Three tons of coal with an ash content of 10% will yield a weight of ash of MOST NEARLY _____ lbs.

   A. 400  B. 500  C. 600  D. 700

   9.___

10. To clean and spread the coal over the grates of a coal-fired boiler, you would use a tool known as a(n)

    A. hoe    B. extractor    C. lance    D. slice bar

11. To burn the volatile matter in coal MORE efficiently, one should

    A. mix peat with the coal
    B. supply overfire draft
    C. mix it with a lower grade of coal
    D. add moisture to the coal

12. The one of the following that lists the size classifications of anthracite coal in proper order ranging from the smallest to the largest is:

    A. Chestnut, culm, pea, birdseye, egg
    B. Egg, stove, pea, broken, culm
    C. Stove, egg, birdseye, culm, broken
    D. Birdseye, pea, chestnut, stove, egg

13. The fire in a hand-fired furnace can be cleaned by a method known as

    A. ashpit to grate         B. bottom to top
    C. side to side            D. grate to crown

14. Coal is normally *tempered* when operating a chain-grate stoker for the purpose of

    A. increasing coking       B. preventing clinking
    C. collecting particles    D. promoting uniform burning

15. The one of the following coals that can legally be burned in power plants is

    A. anthracite              B. sub-bituminous
    C. non-coking              D. bituminous

16. The one of the following that is known as *rice coal* is _____ coal.

    A. pea    B. buckwheat #2    C. egg    D. culm

17. A MAJOR cause of air pollution resulting from the burning of fuel oils is _____ dioxide.

    A. sulphur    B. silicon    C. nitrous    D. hydrogen

18. The $CO_2$ percentage in the flue gas of a power plant is indicated by a

    A. Doppler meter           B. Ranarex indicator
    C. microtector             D. hygrometer

19. The MOST likely cause of black smoke exhausting from the chimney of an oil-fired boiler is

    A. high secondary air flow    B. low stack emission
    C. low oil temperature        D. high chimney draft

20. The diameter of the steam piston in a steam-driven duplex vacuum pump whose dimensions are given as 3 by 2 by 4 is

    A. 2    B. 3    C. 4    D. 6

21. An induced draft fan is GENERALLY connected between the

    A. condenser and the first pass
    B. stack and the breeching
    C. feedwater heater and the boiler feed pump
    D. combustion chamber and fuel oil tanks

22. The PURPOSE of an air chamber on a reciprocating water pump is to

    A. maintain a uniform flow
    B. reduce the amount of steam expansion
    C. create a pulsating flow
    D. vary the amount of steam admission

23. *Flash point* is the temperature at which oil will

    A. change completely to vapor
    B. safely fire in a furnace
    C. flash into flame if a lighted match is passed just above the top of the oil
    D. burn intermittently when ignited

24. A *sounding box* would NORMALLY be found

    A. on top of the boiler
    B. next to a compressed air tank
    C. in a fuel oil tank
    D. in a steam condenser

25. An *intercooler* is GENERALLY found on a(n)

    A. steam pump                B. air compressor
    C. steam engine              D. rotary oil pump

26. The instrument used to measure atmospheric pressure is a

    A. capillary tube            B. venturi
    C. barometer                 D. calorimeter

27. The control which starts or stops the operation of the oil burner at a pre-determined steam pressure is the

    A. pressuretrol              B. air flow interlock
    C. transformer               D. magnetic oil valve

28. In a closed feedwater heater, the water and the steam

    A. come into direct contact
    B. are kept apart from each other
    C. are under negative pressure
    D. mix and exhaust to the atmosphere

29. A *knocking* noise in steam lines is GENERALLY the result of

    A. superheated steam expansion
    B. high steam pressure

C. condensation in the line
D. rapid steam expansion

30. An electrical component known as a step-up transformer operates by   30._____

    A. raising voltage and decreasing amperage
    B. decreasing amperage and raising resistance
    C. raising amperage and decreasing resistance
    D. raising voltage and amperage at the same time

31. A monometer is an instrument that is used to measure   31._____

    A. heat radiation            B. air volume
    C. eondensate water level    D. air pressure

32. Three 75-gallon per hour mechanical pressure type oil burners operating together are to   32._____
    burn 150,000 gallons of No. 6 fuel oil.
    The number of hours they would take to burn this amount of oil is MOST NEARLY

    A. 665        B. 760        C. 870        D. 1210

33. The sum of 10 1/2, 8 3/4, 5 1/2, and 2 1/4 is   33._____

    A. 23         B. 25         C. 26         D. 27

34. A water tank measures 50 feet long, 16 feet wide, and 12 feet high. Assume that water   34._____
    weighs 60 pounds per cubic foot and that one gallon of water weighs 8 pounds.
    The number of gallons the tank can hold when it is half full is

    A. 21,500     B. 28,375     C. 33,410     D. 36,000

35. Assuming 70 gallons of oil cost $42.00, then 110 gallons of oil at the same rate will cost   35._____

    A. $66.00     B. $84.00     C. $96.00     D. $152.00

Questions 36-40.

DIRECTIONS:   Questions 36 through 40, inclusive, are to be answered in accordance with the
              information contained in the following paragraph.

*Fuel is conserved when a boiler is operating near its most efficient load. The efficiency of
a boiler will change as the output varies. Large amounts of air must be used at low ratings
and so the heat exchanger is inefficient. As the output increases, the efficiency decreases
due to an increase in flue gas temperature. Every boiler has an output rate for which its efficiency is highest. For example, in a water-tube boiler, the highest efficiency might occur at
120 percent of rated capacity while in a vertical fire-tube boiler highest efficiency might be at
70% of rated capacity. The type of fuel burned and cleanliness affects the maximum efficiency of the boiler. When a power plant contains a battery of boilers, a sufficient number
should be kept in operation so as to maintain the output of individual units near their points of
maximum efficiency. One of the boilers in the battery can be used as a regulator to meet the
change in demand for steam while the other boilers could still operate at their most efficient
rating. Boiler performance is expressed as the number of pounds of steam generated per
pound of fuel.*

36. According to the above paragraph, the number of pounds of steam generated per pound of fuel is a measure of boiler

    A. size
    B. performance
    C. regulator input
    D. by-pass

37. According to the above paragraph, the HIGHEST efficiency of a vertical fire-tube boiler might occur at

    A. 70% of rate capacity
    B. 80% of water tube capacity
    C. 95% of water tube capacity
    D. 120% of rated capacity

38. According to the above paragraph, the MAXIMUM efficiency of a boiler is affected by

    A. atmospheric temperature
    B. atmospheric pressure
    C. cleanliness
    D. fire brick material

39. According to the above paragraph, a heat exchanger uses large amounts of air at low

    A. fuel rates
    B. ratings
    C. temperatures
    D. pressures

40. According to the above paragraph, one boiler in a battery of boilers should be used as a

    A. demand
    B. stand by
    C. regulator
    D. safety

---

# KEY (CORRECT ANSWERS)

| | | | | | | | |
|---|---|---|---|---|---|---|---|
| 1. | D | 11. | B | 21. | B | 31. | D |
| 2. | C | 12. | D | 22. | A | 32. | A |
| 3. | B | 13. | C | 23. | C | 33. | D |
| 4. | A | 14. | D | 24. | C | 34. | D |
| 5. | D | 15. | A | 25. | B | 35. | A |
| 6. | A | 16. | B | 26. | C | 36. | B |
| 7. | A | 17. | A | 27. | A | 37. | A |
| 8. | C | 18. | B | 28. | B | 38. | C |
| 9. | C | 19. | C | 29. | C | 39. | B |
| 10. | A | 20. | B | 30. | A | 40. | C |

# TEST 3

DIRECTIONS: Each question or incomplete statement is followed by several suggested answers or completions. Select the one that BEST answers the question or completes the statement. *PRINT THE LETTER OF THE CORRECT ANSWER IN THE SPACE AT THE RIGHT.*

1. The bottom blowdown on a boiler is used to

    A. remove mud drum water impurities
    B. increase boiler priming
    C. reduce steam pressure in the header
    D. increase the boiler water level

    1._____

2. The term *spalling* refers to a boiler

    A. flue gas content
    C. combustion chamber
    B. soot blower
    D. mud leg

    2._____

3. The wrench that would NORMALLY be used on hexagonally-shaped screwed valves and fittings is the _____ wrench.

    A. adjustable pipe
    C. monkey
    B. tappet
    D. open-end

    3._____

4. The designated size of a boiler tube is GENERALLY based upon its

    A. internal diameter
    C. wall thickness
    B. external diameter
    D. weight per foot of length

    4._____

5. A fusible plug on a boiler is made PRIMARILY of

    A. selenium    B. tin    C. zinc    D. iron

    5._____

6. The range of *Ph* values for boiler feed water is NORMALLY

    A. 1 to 2    B. 4 to 6    C. 9 to 10    D. 12 to 15

    6._____

7. The *boiler horsepower* is defined as the evaporation of _____ lbs. of water from and at 212° F.

    A. 900    B. 400    C. 345    D. 34.5

    7._____

8. A low pressure air-atomizing oil burner has an operating air pressure range of _____ lbs.

    A. 25 to 35    B. 16 to 20    C. 6 to 10    D. 1 to 2

    8._____

9. A superheater is installed in a Stirling boiler MAINLY for the purpose of raising the temperature of the

    A. secondary air
    B. steam leaving the steam drum
    C. boiler feed water
    D. primary air

    9._____

10. The function of a counterflow economizer in a power plant is to

    A. use flue gases to heat feed water
    B. raise flue gas temperatures
    C. recirculate exhaust steam
    D. pre-heat combustion air

11. A fire due to spontaneous combustion would MOST easily occur in a pile of

    A. asbestos sheathing      B. loose lumber
    C. oil drums               D. oily waste rags

12. A *damper regulator,* used for combustion control, is operated by

    A. steam pressure          B. the water column
    C. the boiler pump         D. a pitot tube

13. The packing of an expansion joint in a firebrick wall of a combustion chamber is GENERALLY made of

    A. silica                  B. brick cement
    C. silicon carbide         D. asbestos

14. An open-ended steam pipe, called a steam lance, is USUALLY used on a boiler to

    A. remove soot             B. bleed the steam header
    C. clean the mud drum      D. clean chimneys

15. A high vacuum reading on the fuel oil gauge would indicate

    A. an empty oil tank       B. high oil temperature
    C. a clogged strainer      D. worn pump gears

16. The one of the following boilers that is classified as an internally-fired boiler is the _____ boiler.

    A. cross-drum straight tube
    B. vertical tubular
    C. Stirling
    D. cross-drum horizontal box-header

17. Try-cocks are used on a boiler PRIMARILY to

    A. check the gauge glass reading
    B. release steam pressure
    C. drain the water column
    D. blow down the gauge glass

18. Scale deposits on the tubes and shell of a high-pressure boiler are UNDESIRABLE because the deposits cause

    A. protrusions or roughness   B. suction
    C. foaming                    D. concentrates

19. The function of a radiation pyrometer is to measure

    A. boiler water height     B. boiler pressure
    C. furnace temperature     D. boiler drum stresses

20. An engine indicator is GENERALLY used to measure

    A. steam temperature
    B. heat losses
    C. errors in gauge readings
    D. steam cylinder pressures

21. A goose-neck is installed in the line connecting a steam gauge to a boiler to

    A. maintain constant steam flow
    B. prevent steam knocking
    C. maintain steam pressure
    D. protect the gauge element

22. A boiler steam gauge should have a range of AT LEAST

    A. one-half the working steam pressure
    B. the working steam pressure
    C. 1 1/2 times the maximum allowable working pressure
    D. twice the maximum allowable working pressure

23. A disconnected steam pressure gauge is USUALLY calibrated with a(n)

    A. Orsat instrument
    B. air pump
    C. tuyeres
    D. dead-weight tester

24. The recommended size joint for repairing firebrick wall is MOST NEARLY

    A. 1/64"    B. 1/16"    C. 1/4"    D. 1/2"

25. The acidity of boiler water is USUALLY determined by a _____ test.

    A. Rockwell
    B. soap hardness
    C. paper
    D. alkalinity

26. Electrostatic precipitators are used in power plants to

    A. remove fly ash from flue gases
    B. measure smoke conditions
    C. collect boiler impurities
    D. disperse minerals in feed water

27. Fly ash from the flue gases in a power plant is collected by a

    A. soot blower
    B. gas separator
    C. stack regulator
    D. mechanical separator

28. The installation of four new split packing rings in a stuffing box requires that the joints of the packing rings be placed _____ apart.

    A. 180°    B. 90°    C. 60°    D. 30°

29. In power plants, boiler feed water is chemically treated in order to

    A. prevent scale formation
    B. increase water foaming
    C. increase oxygen formation
    D. increase the temperature of the water

30. The soot in a fire tube boiler GENERALLY settles on the
    A. bridgewall
    B. inside tube surface
    C. combustion chamber sides
    D. outside tube surface

31. The one of the following classifications of fuel oil strainers that is generally NOT used with the heavier industrial fuel oils is a _____ strainer.
    A. wire mesh
    B. metallic disc
    C. filter cloth
    D. perforated metal cylinder

32. The temperature of the fuel oil leaving a pre-heater is controlled by a(n)
    A. potentiometer
    B. relay
    C. low water cut-off
    D. aquastat

33. A pneumatic tool is GENERALLY powered by
    A. natural gas    B. steam    C. a battery    D. air

34. The maximum steam pressure permitted in the steam coils used for heating the oil in a submerged oil storage tank is MOST NEARLY _____ psi.
    A. 40    B. 35    C. 25    D. 10

35. The water pressure used in a hydrostatic test on a boiler is GENERALLY _____ maximum working pressure.
    A. 4 times
    B. 2 times the
    C. 1 1/2 times the
    D. the same as

36. The one of the following valves that should be used in a steam line to throttle the flow is the _____ valve.
    A. plug    B. check    C. gate    D. globe

37. The CO (carbon monoxide) content in the flue gas from an efficiently fired boiler should be APPROXIMATELY
    A. 0% to 1%
    B. 4% to 6%
    C. 8% to 10%
    D. 12% to 13%

38. The $CO_2$ (carbon dioxide) percentage in the flue gas of an efficiently fired boiler should be APPROXIMATELY
    A. 1%    B. 12%    C. 18%    D. 25%

39. When the temperature of stack gases rises considerably above the normal operating stack temperature, it GENERALLY indicates
    A. a low boiler water level
    B. a heavy smoke condition in the stack
    C. that the boiler is operating efficiently
    D. that the boiler tubes are dirty

40. A boiler safety valve is USUALLY set above the maximum working pressure by an amount equal to _____ of the maximum working pressure.  40._____

    A. 6%   B. 10%   C. 12%   D. 14%

---

# KEY (CORRECT ANSWERS)

| | | | |
|---|---|---|---|
| 1. A | 11. D | 21. D | 31. C |
| 2. C | 12. A | 22. C | 32. D |
| 3. D | 13. D | 23. D | 33. D |
| 4. B | 14. A | 24. B | 34. D |
| 5. B | 15. C | 25. D | 35. C |
| 6. C | 16. B | 26. A | 36. D |
| 7. D | 17. A | 27. D | 37. A |
| 8. D | 18. A | 28. B | 38. B |
| 9. B | 19. C | 29. A | 39. D |
| 10. A | 20. D | 30. B | 40. A |

# EXAMINATION SECTION
# TEST 1

DIRECTIONS: Each question or incomplete statement is followed by several suggested answers or completions. Select the one that BEST answers the question or completes the statement. *PRINT THE LETTER OF THE CORRECT ANSWER IN THE SPACE AT THE RIGHT.*

1. The MAIN function of a *steam separator* in a steam power plant is to

    A. reduce steam pressure
    B. remove excess oil vapors from the steam
    C. increase steam quality
    D. reduce back-pressure on the steam-driven equipment

2. The MAIN purpose of a *dip tube* in a low-pressure hot water system is to

    A. prevent air from entering the main
    B. determine the level of water in the boiler
    C. reduce air pollution
    D. eliminate condensation when starting up

3. The rating of a unit ventilator is USUALLY determined by a(n)

    A. anemometer            B. hydrometer
    C. psychrometer          D. ammeter

4. Of the following devices, the one that is used to record the air-flow-steam-flow relationship of a boiler in a steam plant is a

    A. Orsat analyzer        B. manometer
    C. steam-flow meter      D. heat meter

5. Of the following types of gas fuels, the one which has the HIGHEST BTU content per cubic foot is _____ gas.

    A. manufactured          B. coke-oven
    C. liquid petroleum      D. natural

6. Of the following gasket materials, the one which is BEST to use when oil at 300° F is being carried in a pipe is

    A. fiber and paper       B. synthetic rubber
    C. asbestos composition  D. corrugated copper

7. A monolithic repair of a slightly damaged sectional magnesia insulation covering is BEST made by

    A. wiring in a *Dutchman* and filling the voids with magnesia cement
    B. covering the damaged area with asbestos laminations
    C. filling in the broken portion with glass-fiber insulating cement
    D. replacing the entire section

8. Of the following piping materials, the one that should NOT be used in a fuel-oil piping system is

   A. galvanized iron
   B. type K copper tubing
   C. brass pipe
   D. steel pipe

9. A valve is marked *300 WOG.*
   This valve could NOT be properly used in a pipe conveying _____ pounds gage maximum.

   A. oil at 300
   B. air at 100
   C. water at 150
   D. steam at 300

10. A steam gage connection for a large boiler is connected to the top of the water column and is then brought down to the operating level 24 feet below. The gage actually reads 605 psi.
    The ACTUAL gage pressure in the boiler is MOST NEARLY _____ psi.

    A. 590    B. 595    C. 610    D. 620

11. Of the following types of industrial oil burners, the one that is COMPLETELY adaptable to fully automatic operation or wide variations in firing rate is the _____ burner.

    A. mechanical-pressure type
    B. air-atomizing
    C. steam-atomizing
    D. horizontal rotary-cup

12. A full backward curve type centrifugal fan is being used in a coal-fired power plant for forced draft. Assume that after adjusting the speed of the fan, it is still too high, resulting in more pressure than is necessary to overcome the resistance of the fuel bed and boiler. To correct this situation, it would be BEST to replace the fan with one of a _____ diameter, running at _____ rpm and with a _____ wheel.

    A. *smaller;* greater; *wider*
    B. *larger;* less; *wider*
    C. *larger;* greater; *smaller*
    D. *smaller;* less; *smaller*

13. Short stroking in a steam-driven reciprocating pump results in both a(n) _____ in steam consumption and a(n) _____ in pumping capacity.

    A. *decrease;* decrease
    B. *increase;* increase
    C. *decrease;* increase
    D. *increase;* decrease

14. Caustic embrittlement is the weakening of boiler steel as the result of inner crystalline cracks.
    This condition is caused by BOTH long exposure to

    A. a combination of stress and highly acidic water
    B. stress in the presence of free oxygen and highly acidic water
    C. a combination of stress and water with a pH of 7
    D. a combination of stress and highly alkaline water

15. Of the following statements pertaining to feedwater injectors, the one which is MOST nearly correct is that the injectors

    A. are very efficient pumping units
    B. are practical only on small boilers
    C. are very reliable in operation on all types of boilers
    D. can handle 250 to 300 degree water

15.____

16. In reference to power plant pumps, the letters N.P.S.H. are an abbreviation for

    A. Non Positive Static Head
    B. Net Position Static Head
    C. Non Positive Standard Head
    D. Net Positive Suction Head

16.____

17. A pump's maintenance is based on a preventive maintenance schedule. This means that the schedule should GENERALLY be determined by the

    A. actual time lapse between maintenance checks
    B. actual number of pump-operating hours
    C. pump's actual operating performance
    D. operating performance of the equipment connected to the pump

17.____

18. Periodic inspection and testing of mechanical equipment by the staff at a plant is done MAINLY to

    A. help the men to better understand the operation of the equipment
    B. keep the men busy during slack times
    C. encourage the men to better understand each others' working capabilities
    D. discover minor equipment faults before they develop into major breakdowns

18.____

19. In planning a preventive maintenance program, the FIRST step to be taken is to

    A. repair all equipment that is not in service
    B. check all fuel oil burner tips
    C. make an inventory of all plant equipment
    D. check all electrical wiring to motors

19.____

20. An electric motor having class A insulation has been permitted to operate continuously at rated load even though the internal insulation temperature reads 10C above the allowable maximum internal temperature. Operating at this excessive temperature WOULD

    A. require frequent lubrication of the motor bearings
    B. reduce the life expectancy of the electric motor
    C. require an increase in voltage
    D. reduce the power factor to one-half of its normal value

20.____

21. The synchronous speed of a three-phase squirrel cage induction motor operating from a fixed frequency system can ONLY be changed by altering the

    A. rated locked-rotor torque
    B. rheostat position of the unloaded machine
    C. brush holder position
    D. number of poles in the stator

21.____

22. A thermal overload relay on an electric motor has been frequently tripping out.
Of the following actions, the BEST one to take first to correct this problem would be to

    A. bypass the relay
    B. block the relay on a closed position
    C. clean the relay contacts
    D. arbitrarily readjust the relay setting

23. An air heater for a steam generator providing combustion air at temperatures ranging upward from 300F will often effect savings in fuel ranging from

    A. 1 to 3%   B. 5 to 10%   C. 12 to 15%   D. 17 to 20%

24. You have been asked to make an inspection of the superheater of a steam generator for external corrosion. You should be aware that if the direction of gas flow perpendicular to a tangent to the superheater tube is considered to be the 12 o'clock position, the GREATEST metal loss due to external corrosion usually occurs on the _____ o'clock and _____ o'clock sectors of the tube.

    A. 12; 6   B. 10; 2   C. 8; 3   D. 7; 5

25. In the steam generating plant to which you are assigned, the starting-up time and the shutting-down time for the boiler is determined by the time required to limit the thermal stresses in the drums and headers. The drums and headers have rolled tube joints. The temperature change in saturated temperature per hour for limit controlled heating and cooling rates for this boiler is established at _____ change.

    A. 50° F   B. 75° F   C. 100° F   D. 200° F

## KEY (CORRECT ANSWERS)

| | | | |
|---|---|---|---|
| 1. C | | 11. D | |
| 2. A | | 12. B | |
| 3. A | | 13. D | |
| 4. C | | 14. D | |
| 5. C | | 15. B | |
| 6. C | | 16. D | |
| 7. A | | 17. B | |
| 8. A | | 18. D | |
| 9. D | | 19. C | |
| 10. B | | 20. B | |

21. D
22. C
23. B
24. B
25. C

# TEST 2

DIRECTIONS: Each question or incomplete statement is followed by several suggested answers or completions. Select the one that BEST answers the question or completes the statement. *PRINT THE LETTER OF THE CORRECT ANSWER IN THE SPACE AT THE RIGHT.*

1. Assume that the optimum pH level of boiler feedwater for a boiler installation ranges between 8.0 and 9.5.
   The alkalizer used in the feedwater treatment to maintain this optimum pH level SHOULD introduce

   A. an average amount of iron and copper corrosion products into the steam cycle
   B. an increase of partial pressure of the carbon dioxide in the steam
   C. the least amount of iron and copper corrosion products into the boiler cycle
   D. a control of corrosion rates by forming a coating on the surfaces contacted by the steam

   1._____

2. The ppm of sodium sulfite that can be *safely* used for the chemical scavenging of oxygen in boiler feedwater is DEPENDENT upon the

   A. steam output of the boiler
   B. boiler operating pressure
   C. number of boiler steam drums
   D. construction of the boiler

   2._____

3. Of the following piping materials, the one which is NOT generally used for pneumatic temperature control systems is

   A. copper           B. plastic
   C. steel            D. galvanized iron

   3._____

4. In accordance with recommended maintenance practice, thermostats used in a pneumatic temperature control system SHOULD be checked

   A. weekly           B. bi-monthly
   C. monthly          D. once a year

   4._____

5. Of the following, the BEST method to use to determine the moisture level in a refrigeration system is to

   A. weigh the drier after it has been in the system for a period of time
   B. visually check the sight glass for particles of corrosion
   C. use a moisture indicator
   D. test a sample of lubricating oil with phosphorus pentoxide

   5._____

6. A full-flow drier is USUALLY recommended to be used in a hermetic refrigeration compressor system to keep the system dry and to

   A. prevent the products of decomposition from getting into the evaporator in the event of a motor burn-out
   B. condense cut liquid refrigerant during compressor off cycles and compressor start-up
   C. prevent the compressor unit from decreasing in capacity
   D. prevent the liquid from dumping into the compressor crankcase

   6._____

7. An economizer in a steam boiler is used to raise the temperature of the

   A. combustion air for firing fuel oil utilizing some of the heat in the exit flue gases
   B. combustion air for firing fuel oil utilizing some of the heat in the exhaust steam from the turbines of steam engines
   C. boiler feedwater by utilizing some of the heat in the exit flue gases
   D. boiler feedwater by utilizing some of the heat in the exhaust steam from the turbines or steam engines

8. A mixed-base grease is a grease that is prepared by mixing lubricating oil with

   A. one metallic soap
   B. two metallic soaps
   C. a synthetic lubricant
   D. heavy gear oil

9. Of the following lubricants, the one which is classified as a circulating oil is _____ oil.

   A. turbine
   B. gear
   C. machine
   D. steam-cylinder

10. You are supervising the installation of a steam-driven reciprocating pump. The pump's air chamber is missing and you have to replace it with one with several salvaged ones. The salvaged air chamber selected should have a volume equal to MOST NEARLY _____ the piston displacement of the pump.

    A. half of
    B. 1 1/2 times
    C. 2 times
    D. 2 1/2 times

11. Economical partial-load operation of steam turbines is obtained by minimizing throttling losses.
    This is accomplished by

    A. reducing the boiler pressure and temperature
    B. throttling the steam flow into the uncontrolled set of nozzles
    C. dividing the first-stage nozzles into several groups and providing a steam control valve for each group
    D. controlling the fuel flow to the steam generator

12. You are ordering two pump wearing rings for a centrifugal pump.
    These rings are GENERALLY identified as

    A. two wearing rings
    B. one drive wearing ring and one casing wearing ring
    C. one casing wearing ring and one impeller wearing ring
    D. one first-stage wearing ring and one drive wearing ring

13. A thermo-hydraulic feedwater regulator is used to regulate the flow of water to a drum-type boiler. The amount of water input to the boiler is controlled *in proportion to* the

    A. boiler load
    B. setting of the feed pump relief valve
    C. amount of water in the outer tube that flashes into steam
    D. water level in the drum

14. The standard capacity rating conditions for any refrigeration compressor is _____ psig for the suction and _____ psig for the discharge.   14.____

    A. 5° F, 19.6; 86° F, 154.5
    B. 5° F, 9.6; 96° F, 154.5
    C. 10° F, 9.6; 96° F, 144.5
    D. 10° F, 19.6; 96° F, 134.5

15. Of the following, the MAIN purpose of a subcooler in a refrigerant piping system for a two-stage system is to   15.____

    A. reduce the total power requirements and total heat rejection to the second stage
    B. reduce total power requirements and return oil to the compressor
    C. improve the flow of evaporator gas per ton and increase the temperature
    D. increase the heat rejection per ton and avoid system shutdown

16. In large refrigeration systems, the USUAL location for charging the refrigeration system is into the   16.____

    A. suction line
    B. liquid line between the receiver shut-off valve and the expansion valve
    C. line between the condenser and the compressor
    D. line between the high pressure cut-off switch and the expansion valve

17. The effect of a voltage variation to 90 percent of normal voltage, for a compound wound DC motor, on the FULL load current is   17.____

    A. an increase in the full load current of approximately 10%
    B. a decrease in the full load current of approximately 10%
    C. zero
    D. a decrease in the full load current 20%

18. The purpose of a current-limiting reactor is to place an upper limit on the available short-circuit current that can occur under fault conditions.
    The reactor accomplishes this by contributing _____ to the circuit.   18.____

    A. additional capacitance
    B. reduced inductive reactance
    C. reduced capacitance
    D. additional inductive reactance

19. Alternating current electric motors are usually guaranteed to operate satisfactorily and to deliver their full horsepower PROVIDED the electrical power delivered to the motor is at the rated   19.____

    A. voltage and at plus or minus 5 percent frequency variation
    B. frequency and at a voltage 15 percent above or below rating
    C. voltage and at plus or minus 10 percent frequency variation
    D. frequency and at a voltage 20 percent above or below rating

20. A three-phase AC motor is connected to a 230 volt, three-phase, alternating current line. With this motor running at full load, the line current is found to be 20 amperes, with a power factor of 0.75.
    Under these conditions, the power, in kilowatts, supplied to this motor will be MOST NEARLY   20.____

    A. 3.5
    B. 6.0
    C. 10.5
    D. 18.0

21. In accordance with the air pollution control code, no person shall cause or permit the emission of air contaminants from a boiler with a capacity of 500 million BTU per hour or more, if the air contaminant emitted has a sulfur dioxide content of MORE than _____ parts per million by volume of undiluted emissions measured at _____ percent excess air.

    A. 300; 15  B. 200; 10  C. 200; 15  D. 300; 10

22. Of the following statements concerning the requirements of the air pollution control code, the one which is the MOST complete and correct is that the owner of equipment

    A. and apparatus shall maintain such equipment and apparatus in good operating order by regular inspection and cleaning and by promptly making repairs
    B. shall maintain the equipment in good operating condition by making inspections and repairs on a regular basis
    C. and apparatus shall maintain the equipment and apparatus in operating condition by regular inspection and cleaning
    D. shall maintain such equipment in good working order by regular inspection and cleaning and by making repairs on a scheduled basis

23. Assume that one of your assistants was near the Freon 11 refrigeration system when a liquid Freon line ruptured. Some of the liquid Freon 11 has gotten into your assistant's right eye.
    Of the following actions, the one which you should NOT take is to

    A. immediately call for an eye specialist (medical doctor)
    B. gently and quickly rub the Freon 11 out of the eye
    C. use a boric-acid solution to clean out the Freon 11 from his eye
    D. wash the eye by gently blowing the Freon 11 out of his eye with air

24. Assume that a fire breaks out in an electrical control panel board.
    Of the following types of portable fire extinguishers, the BEST one to use to put out this fire would be a _____ type.

    A. dry-chemical           B. soda-acid
    C. foam                   D. water-stream

25. Assume that you are checking the water level in a boiler which is on the line in a power plant. Upon opening the gage cocks, you determine that the water level was above the top gage cock.
    Of the following actions, the BEST one to take FIRST in this situation would be to

    A. shut off the fuel and air supply
    B. surface-blow the boiler
    C. close the steam-outlet valve from the boiler
    D. increase the speed of the feedwater pump

# KEY (CORRECT ANSWERS)

| | | | |
|---|---|---|---|
| 1. | C | 11. | C |
| 2. | B | 12. | C |
| 3. | C | 13. | D |
| 4. | D | 14. | A |
| 5. | C | 15. | A |
| 6. | A | 16. | B |
| 7. | C | 17. | A |
| 8. | B | 18. | D |
| 9. | A | 19. | A |
| 10. | D | 20. | B |

21. B
22. A
23. B
24. A
25. C

---

# EXAMINATION SECTION
# TEST 1

DIRECTIONS: Each question or incomplete statement is followed by several suggested answers or completions. Select the one that BEST answers the question or completes the statement. *PRINT THE LETTER OF THE CORRECT ANSWER IN THE SPACE AT THE RIGHT.*

1. Of the following, the one that is an *inherent* boiler heat loss is the loss due to

   A. dry chimney gases
   B. excess air
   C. unburned gaseous combustibles
   D. radiation from the furnace setting

2. The one of the following flue gases whose presence indicates that MORE excess air is being supplied to a furnace than is being used is

   A. carbon dioxide      B. carbon monoxide
   C. nitrogen            D. oxygen

3. A pressure gage on a compressed air tank reads 35.3 psi at 70° F.
   If, due to a fire, the temperature of the air in the tank were to increase to 600° F, the gage reading should be MOST NEARLY _____ psi.

   A. 70      B. 75      C. 80      D. 85

4. Of the following types of flow meters, the one that is MOST accurate is a

   A. concentric orifice      B. venturi tube
   C. flow nozzle             D. pitot tube

5. A spring pop safety valve on a fired high-pressure boiler fails to pop at its set pressure. Which of the following methods should be used to free the valve before retesting it?

   A. Strike the valve body with a soft lead hammer until it pops
   B. Raise the valve lifting-lever and release it
   C. Reduce the spring compression gradually until the valve opens
   D. Unscrew the valve one-quarter turn to relieve the strain on it

6. A device which retains the desired parts of a steam-and-water mixture while rejecting the undesired parts of the mixture is a

   A. check valve      B. calorimeter
   C. stud tube        D. steam trap

7. The MAIN advantage of using water-tube boilers in preference to fire-tube boilers in an installation is that water-tube boilers can be

   A. built much larger
   B. equipped with superheaters
   C. stoker-fired
   D. made portable

8. The PRIMARY purpose of using phosphate to treat boiler water is to

   A. precipitate the hardness constituents
   B. scavenge the dissolved oxygen
   C. dissolve the calcium
   D. dissolve the magnesium

9. Assume that the set pressure of a safety valve on a power boiler is 100 psi. The MINIMUM pressure at which the safety valve must close after blowing down is _____ psi.

   A. 92     B. 94     C. 96     D. 98

10. A one-pound sample of wet steam at a certain pressure has an enthalpy of 960 BTU. For this same pressure, the Steam Tables list the enthalpy of saturated liquid as 130 and of saturated vapor as 1130 BTU.
    The quality of the sample steam is MOST NEARLY

    A. 75%    B. 85%    C. 90%    D. 95%

11. The type of feedwater heater which uses hot flue gases to heat the feedwater is known as a(n)

    A. economizer              B. direct-contact heater
    C. deaerator               D. surface heater

12. The minimum recommended suction head for a centrifugal pump handling feedwater at 300° F is 155 feet.
    If the vapor pressure corresponding to the water temperature is 135 feet and the losses in the suction piping amount to 5 feet, the pump should be located AT LEAST _____ the lowest level of the water in the heater.

    A. 25 feet below           B. 15 feet below
    C. 15 feet above           D. 25 feet above

13. As compared to a power-driven triplex single-acting pump of the same size and operating at the same speed, a steam-driven duplex double-acting pump will

    A. pump more water per minute
    B. give a more uniform discharge
    C. have a higher first cost
    D. be more economical to operate

14. The MAIN advantage of operating a steam engine or steam turbine *condensing* is that it

    A. increases the mean effective pressure in the prime mover
    B. decreases the condensate temperature
    C. permits the use of exhaust steam to drive auxiliary equipment
    D. eliminates the need for separating non-condensibles from the steam

15. The automatic shut-off valves for a water gage installed on a high-pressure boiler must be _____ check valves.

    A. horizontal swing        B. vertical swing
    C. ball                    D. spring-loaded

16. The efficiency of a riveted joint is defined as the ratio of the 16.____

    A. plate thickness to the rivet diameter
    B. strength of the riveted joint to the strength of a welded joint
    C. strength of the riveted joint to the strength of the solid plate
    D. number of rivets in the first row of the joint to the total number of rivets on one side of the joint

17. A pump delivers 1500 pounds of water per minute against a total head of 200 feet. The water horsepower of this pump is MOST NEARLY 17.____

    A. 10   B. 40   C. 100   D. 600

18. In the most usual type of large capacity oil burner using #6 oil, under *fully automatic* control, the atomization of the oil is produced MAINLY by the 18.____

    A. pressure from the pump
    B. pressure from the secondary air fan
    C. oil temperature from the heater
    D. rotation of the burner assembly by the motor

19. Which of the following comes the closest to indicating the number of degree-days in a normal heating season in the city? 19.____

    A. 3000   B. 4000   C. 5000   D. 6000

20. In which of the following methods of steam generation would you expect to obtain reasonably continuous values of $CO_2$ CLOSEST to the perfect $CO_2$ value? 20.____
    Automatic

    A. stoker firing with temperature recorder
    B. stoker firing with *hold fire timer*
    C. oil firing with *stack switch*
    D. oil firing with *haze regulator*

21. The loss of heat in stack gases for heavy fuel oils is HIGHEST when the $CO_2$ content is 21.____
    _____ and the stack temperature is _____.

    A. 12%; 500°   B. 8%; 600°   C. 6%; 700°   D. 14%; 600°

22. A badly sooted HRT boiler under coal firing will show a _____ than a clean boiler. 22.____

    A. *higher* $CO_2$ value
    B. *lower* $CO_2$ value
    C. *higher* stack temperature
    D. *lower* draft loss

23. A unit heater condensing 50 lbs. of low pressure steam per hour would be rated MOST NEARLY at _____ square feet E.D.R. 23.____

    A. 50   B. 100   C. 150   D. 200

24. Which of the following values MOST NEARLY equals one horsepower? 24.____

    A. 550 ft.lbs. per sec.
    B. 3300 ft.lbs. per min.
    C. 5500 ft.lbs. per hour
    D. 10000 ft.lbs. per min.

25. An indicator card from a steam engine is most useful to the engineer in  25.____
    A. determining the boiler pressure
    B. determining the engine speed
    C. adjusting the valve setting
    D. computing the mechanical efficiency

---

## KEY (CORRECT ANSWERS)

1. A
2. D
3. D
4. B
5. B

6. D
7. A
8. A
9. C
10. B

11. A
12. A
13. A
14. A
15. C

16. C
17. A
18. D
19. C
20. D

21. C
22. C
23. D
24. A
25. C

---

# TEST 2

DIRECTIONS: Each question or incomplete statement is followed by several suggested answers or completions. Select the one that BEST answers the question or completes the statement. *PRINT THE LETTER OF THE CORRECT ANSWER IN THE SPACE AT THE RIGHT.*

1. A centrifugal water pump is direct-driven by a 25 HP 900 RPM electric motor at rated load.
   In order to double the quantity of water delivered, it would be necessary to substitute a motor rated at _____ HP at _____ RPM.

   A. 40; 1200   B. 50; 1200   C. 100; 1800   D. 200; 1800

   1.____

2. The angle of advance of the eccentric on a D-slide valve steam engine is equal to

   A. the lead angle minus the lap angle
   B. the lead angle plus the lap angle
   C. 90 degrees minus the lead angle
   D. 90 degrees plus the lead and the lap angle

   2.____

3. Of the following statements pertaining to a duplex steam-driven water pump, the one which is NOT true is that

   A. the slide valves have a steam and an exhaust lap
   B. there is a pause in the flow of water through the discharge valve at the end of the stroke
   C. the piston stroke can be adjusted
   D. an air chamber may be omitted on small sizes

   3.____

4. The diagram on which a steam throttling process is indicated by a straight horizontal line is the _____ diagram.

   A. PV             B. Mollier
   C. Ringelman      D. temperature-entropy

   4.____

5. The one of the following devices which is useful in preventing damage to a multi-stage turbine rotor due to unequal thermal expansion or contraction is the

   A. thrust bearing
   B. dummy piston and seal
   C. rupture seal
   D. motor-driven turning gear

   5.____

6. The purpose of a steam turbine's governing system is to control steam flow through the unit, usually in order to keep some other factor constant.
   When a steam turbine is driving an alternator, the factor which is usually kept constant by the governor's operation is the

   A. inlet steam pressure      B. exhaust steam pressure
   C. shaft speed               D. power output

   6.____

7. The speed regulation of a condensing steam turbine operating at 1800 RPM at no load and 1750 RPM at full load is MOST NEARLY

   A. 1%   B. 3%   C. 5%   D. 7%

   7.____

8. The one of the following statements which is NOT true of the operation of steam turbines is that they

    A. operate most efficiently at high speed
    B. can be operated condensing or non-condensing
    C. can be used to drive centrifugal water pumps
    D. need high viscosity cylinder oil mixed with the steam supply to operate properly

9. Of the following, the one which is TRUE regarding backpressure steam turbines is that they

    A. operate on the exhaust steam from higher pressure turbines
    B. operate condensing
    C. exhaust through a very large hood
    D. convert a small part of the available heat in the steam into power

10. An aftercooler on a reciprocating air compressor is used PRIMARILY to

    A. increase compressor capacity
    B. improve compressor efficiency
    C. condense the moisture in the compressed air
    D. cool the lubricating oil

11. The one of the following tasks which is an example of preventive maintenance is

    A. replacing a leaking water pipe nipple
    B. cleaning the cup on a rotary cup burner
    C. cleaning a completely clogged oil strainer
    D. replacing a blown fuse

12. The four MAIN causes of failure of three-phase electric motors are

    A. dirt, friction, moisture, single-phasing
    B. friction, moisture, single-phasing, vibration
    C. dirt, moisture, single-phasing, vibration
    D. dirt, friction, moisture, vibration

13. Assume that an alternator running at a speed of 1800 RPM generates AC voltage at a frequency of 60 cycles per second (Hertz).
    The number of poles in this alternator is

    A. 2        B. 4        C. 6        D. 8

14. Assume that on an integrating watt-hour meter with 4 dials, the respective pointers from left to right are between 7 and 8, between 5 and 6, between 0 and 1, and between 3 and 4.
    Under these conditions, the reading is

    A. 8614        B. 7503        C. 3168        D. 3067

15. Assume that an ammeter is properly connected to a current transformer that has a ratio of 80 to 5. When the ammeter indicates 4.0 amperes, the current in the primary circuit is MOST NEARLY _____ amperes.

    A. 4.0        B. 20.0        C. 64.0        D. 80.0

16. Assume that two alternators, No. 1 and No. 2, are operating in parallel and that alternator No. 1 is taking a greater share of the load than alternator No. 2.
    Of the following, the PROPER method to reapportion the load between the two alternators is to

    A. speed up No. 2
    B. slow down No. 1
    C. increase the excitation of No. 2
    D. adjust the governors of both prime movers

    16.____

17. Which of the following CORRECTLY describes the flow of electric power in a three-phase alternator?
    The input is _____ and the output is _____.

    A. three-phase AC to the stator; single-phase AC from the rotor
    B. three-phase AC to the rotor; single-phase AC from the stator
    C. DC to the stator; three-phase AC from the rotor
    D. DC to the rotor; three-phase AC from the stator

    17.____

18. When the load on a mechanical stoker fired boiler plant furnishing steam for slide valve engine generators drops by 30%, the

    A. stoker should be shut down
    B. fan should be speeded up and the stoker slowed
    C. stoker should be speeded up and the air supply reduced
    D. stoker speed and air supply should be adjusted by reducing both

    18.____

19. Which of the following statements is MOST NEARLY correct?

    A. All types of mechanical stokers may be used with equal efficiency under all types of boilers.
    B. Most stokers are designed with a weak member.
    C. The best type of stoker to use is not dependent upon the type of fuel available.
    D. The advisability of installing stokers is not dependent upon the load.

    19.____

20. The number and size of safety valves required on a high pressure boiler is dependent upon the

    A. size of the boiler drums
    B. amount of heating surface
    C. number of pounds of fuel burned per square foot of grate per hour
    D. size of the steam main

    20.____

21. In changing over a boiler from high pressure (150 lbs. per square inch) to 10 lbs. per square inch, it is USUALLY necessary to

    A. *increase* the size of the safety valves
    B. *decrease* the grate area
    C. *increase* the size of the feedwater piping
    D. *increase* the size of the blow down piping

    21.____

22. A boiler feed injector becomes temporarily steam bound. To correct this condition, the MOST proper action to take is to

    A. increase boiler pressure
    B. reduce suction lift
    C. wrap it with cold rags
    D. bank fire

23. If in your plant the volume of air in cu.ft. per min. for combustion is represented by X, which of the following lowing values of X would MOST NEARLY represent the Cfm of stack gas, under usual conditions, that an induced draft fan would have to handle?

    A. X    B. 2X    C. 3X    D. 4X

24. If the stack switch of an oil burner becomes excessively sooted, a condition that is MOST likely to result is

    A. continuous shutting down of the burner shortly after it starts up
    B. excessive flow of oil to the burner resulting in a smoky fire
    C. excessive fire due to failure to cut off current to the burner motor
    D. failure of the warp switch of the relay to operate

25. In the usual high pressure electric generating plant in large buildings, heating the feedwater from 70° F to 180° F with exhaust steam usually will *decrease* the fuel consumption by

    A. 5%    B. 10%    C. 15%    D. 20%

---

# KEY (CORRECT ANSWERS)

| | | | |
|---|---|---|---|
| 1. D | | 11. B | |
| 2. B | | 12. D | |
| 3. A | | 13. B | |
| 4. B | | 14. B | |
| 5. D | | 15. C | |
| 6. C | | 16. D | |
| 7. B | | 17. D | |
| 8. D | | 18. D | |
| 9. D | | 19. B | |
| 10. C | | 20. B | |

21. A
22. C
23. B
24. A
25. B

# EXAMINATION SECTION
## TEST 1

DIRECTIONS: Each question or incomplete statement is followed by several suggested answers or completions. Select the one that BEST answers the question or completes the statement. *PRINT THE LETTER OF THE CORRECT ANSWER IN THE SPACE AT THE RIGHT.*

1. The capacity of a water-cooled condenser is LEAST affected by the

    A. surrounding air temperature
    B. water temperature
    C. refrigerant temperature
    D. quantity of water being circulated

2. The type of refrigeration system MOST commonly used in ice-skating rinks is the _____ system.

    A. direct expansion          B. simple secondary
    C. compound secondary        D. quadric resistance

3. The theoretical amount of refrigeration required to freeze one ton of water from 66° F to ice at 28° F in one day is _____ ton(s).

    A. 1.00      B. 1.25      C. 1.50      D. 1.75

4. The brine solution MOST commonly used in ice-skating rink piping, as a freezing medium, is a mixture of water and

    A. calcium chloride          B. sodium chloride
    C. glycol                    D. methanol

5. In an absorption refrigeration system, latent heat is absorbed by the refrigerant in the

    A. evaporator and the generator
    B. evaporator and the absorber
    C. condenser and the absorber
    D. condenser and the generator

6. Of the following refrigerants, the one which has the HIGHEST evaporator pressure at the standard 5° F temperature is

    A. ammonia                   B. freon 12
    C. methyl-chloride           D. carbon dioxide

7. The cooler in a refrigeration system that is equipped with automatic protective devices is MOST likely to be accidentally damaged by water freeze-up when the

    A. system is operating under reduced load
    B. system is operating at rated load
    C. system is being pumped down
    D. condenser cooling water flow is interrupted

8. The one of the following statements pertaining to refrigerant compressor lubricants that is NOT true is that

   A. the type of oil that is used to lubricate centrifugal compressors can also be used in speed increasers
   B. ammonia causes very little viscosity change in lubricating oil
   C. most reciprocating compressors handling ammonia or freons can be lubricated properly with an oil having a viscosity of 300 Sec. SU @ 100° F
   D. freon 12 causes very little viscosity change in lubricating oil

9. The one of the following capacity controls which is USUALLY found in a refrigerant reciprocating-compressor system is a

   A. suction valve unloader
   B. throttling damper
   C. variable inlet guide vane
   D. condenser temperature control

10. A thermostatic expansion valve is connected to an evaporator operating at 5° F and 11.8 psig. The valve is in equilibrium at 10° superheat, and the pressure in the bulb is 17.7 psig.
    The EQUIVALENT valve-spring pressure on the refrigerant side of the sensitive element is _____ psi.

    A. 5.9          B. 10.9          C. 22.8          D. 29.5

11. A pressure gage on a compressed air tank reads 35.3 psi at 70° F.
    If, due to a fire, the temperature of the air in the tank were to increase to 600° F, the gage reading should be MOST NEARLY _____ psi.

    A. 70           B. 75            C. 80            D. 85

12. An ADVANTAGE that variable-speed control of a fan has over damper control is

    A. lower first-cost of controls
    B. lower power consumption
    C. cheaper fan drive motor
    D. constant high efficiency throughout entire fan load range

13. An intercooler is used on a two-stage air compressor to reduce the

    A. cylinder temperature in the first stage
    B. amount of condensate in the second stage
    C. back pressure of the air in the first stage
    D. work done on the air in the second stage

14. Of the following, the BEST instrument to use to measure small pressure differentials at low pressure is the

    A. mercury manometer          B. bourdon tube gage
    C. pressurtrol                D. inclined manometer

15. A modulating pressurtrol on a boiler should contain a 15.____

    A. potentiometer
    B. mercury switch
    C. manual reset lever
    D. level indicator

16. Of the following automatic refrigerant expansion valves, the one which can only be used in a system where the liquid refrigerant can largely be stored in the evaporator without danger of sending slugs of liquid refrigerant over to the compressor is the _____ valve. 16.____

    A. thermal-expansion
    B. diaphragm-expansion
    C. high-side float
    D. low-side float

17. The refrigerating effect of a fluid is measured by the amount of heat it is capable of absorbing from the time it enters the 17.____

    A. evaporator as a liquid and leaves as a vapor
    B. condenser as a vapor and leaves as a liquid
    C. expansion valve as a liquid and leaves as a vapor
    D. compressor as a vapor and leaves as a vapor

18. The one of the following which lists the refrigerants in CORRECT order of decreasing toxicity is: 18.____

    A. Ammonia, sulphur dioxide, freon 12
    B. Sulphur dioxide, ammonia, freon 12
    C. Sulphur dioxide, freon 12, ammonia
    D. Ammonia, freon 12, sulphur dioxide

19. The one of the following methods which would MOST likely be used to control the capacity of a large centrifugal refrigerant compressor is the _____ method. 19.____

    A. cylinder unloader
    B. variable cylinder clearance
    C. variable speed
    D. stop and start

20. On a hot summer day, the GREATEST number of people working in a large air-conditioned office would feel comfortable if the temperature and relative humidity were maintained at 20.____

    A. 77° F and 50%
    B. 80° F and 60%
    C. 74° F and 30%
    D. 71° F and 50%

21. The one of the following conditions which has the GREATEST effect on the suction pressure on a swimming pool circulating pump is a 21.____

    A. clogged hair and lint strainer
    B. loss of coagulant
    C. low pH level
    D. clogged filter

22. A coagulant used in swimming pool filters is 22.____

    A. alum
    B. chlorine
    C. soda-ash
    D. sodium hypochlorite

23. According to the health code, the pH reading of swimming pool water should be between _____ and _____.

    A. 5.8; 6.4    B. 6.8; 7.4    C. 7.8; 8.4    D. 8.8; 9.4

24. An orthotolidine test is made to find out how much of which substance is contained in a sample of water?

    A. Alum    B. Ammonia    C. Chlorine    D. Soda-ash

25. The MINIMUM air temperature which must be maintained in an indoor swimming pool, except during the summer months, is _____ °F.

    A. 68    B. 71    C. 75    D. 82

## KEY (CORRECT ANSWERS)

1. A
2. B
3. B
4. A
5. A

6. D
7. C
8. D
9. A
10. A

11. D
12. B
13. D
14. D
15. A

16. C
17. A
18. B
19. C
20. A

21. A
22. A
23. C
24. C
25. C

# TEST 2

DIRECTIONS: Each question or incomplete statement is followed by several suggested answers or completions. Select the one that BEST answers the question or completes the statement. *PRINT THE LETTER OF THE CORRECT ANSWER IN THE SPACE AT THE RIGHT.*

1. A permit is required for the storage or use of liquid chlorine. This permit is issued by which city agency? The

    A. Health Services Administration
    B. Board of Standards and Appeals
    C. Board of Water Supply
    D. Fire Department

    1.____

2. The MINIMUM amount of free chlorine that swimming pool water should contain for proper disinfection is _____ part(s) per million.

    A. 1.0     B. 10     C. 40     D. 400

    2.____

3. The agency which approves gas masks suitable for use in high concentrations of chlorine gas is the United States

    A. Environmental Protection Agency
    B. Department of Agriculture
    C. Bureau of Mines
    D. Department of Defense

    3.____

4. The daily operational records of swimming pools which are required by the health code must be kept for a period of AT LEAST

    A. one month          B. six months
    C. one year           D. two years

    4.____

5. The one of the following which is NOT used as a filtering media in swimming pool filters is

    A. sand               B. quartz
    C. diatomaceous earth D. clay

    5.____

6. The point at which swimming pool filters should be back-washed is when the difference between the inlet and outlet pressure EXCEEDS _____ psi.

    A. 5      B. 10     C. 15     D. 20

    6.____

7. Of the following valves, the type which can be used to adjust the rate-of-flow in a swimming pool filter is the _____ valve.

    A. butterfly          B. needle
    C. gate               D. stop-and-waste

    7.____

8. When the coagulant in a swimming pool filter fails to jelly, the MOST likely cause of the failure is

    A. high water temperature          B. excess bacteria in the water
    C. insufficient alkalinity of the water  D. excess algae in the water

    8.____

9. Of the following types of flow meters, the one that is MOST accurate is a

   A. concentric orifice
   B. venturi tube
   C. flow nozzle
   D. pitot tube

10. A spring pop safety valve on a fired high-pressure boiler fails to pop at its set pressure. Which of the following methods should be used to free the valve before retesting it?

    A. Strike the valve body with a soft lead hammer until it pops
    B. Raise the valve lifting-lever and release it
    C. Reduce the spring compression gradually until the valve opens
    D. Unscrew the valve one-quarter turn to relieve the strain on it

11. A device which retains the desired parts of a steam and water mixture while rejecting the undesired parts of the mixture is a

    A. check valve
    B. calorimeter
    C. stud tube
    D. steam trap

12. The PRIMARY purpose of using phosphate to treat boiler water is to

    A. precipitate the hardness constituents
    B. scavenge the dissolved oxygen
    C. dissolve the calcium
    D. dissolve the magnesium

13. The efficiency of a riveted joint is defined as the ratio of the

    A. plate thickness to the rivet diameter
    B. strength of the riveted joint to the strength of a welded joint
    C. strength of the riveted joint to the strength of the solid plate
    D. number of rivets in the first row of the joint to the total number of rivets on one side of the joint

14. A pump delivers 1500 pounds of water per minute against a total head of 200 feet. The water horsepower of this pump is MOST NEARLY

    A. 10   B. 40   C. 100   D. 600

15. A centrifugal water pump is direct-driven by a 25 HP 900 RPM electric motor at rated load.
    In order to double the quantity of water delivered, it would be necessary to substitute a motor rated at _____ HP at _____ RPM.

    A. 40; 1200   B. 50; 1200   C. 100; 1800   D. 200; 1800

16. Of the following fire extinguisher ratings, the one which indicates that an extinguisher has the GREATEST capability for extinguishing wood, paper, and electrical fires is

    A. 2-A:16-B:C
    B. 4-A:4-B:C
    C. 16-A
    D. 8-B

17. Of the following combinations of oil burners and fuel oils, the combination which is the MOST hazardous to fire-up when placing a cold boiler into service is the

    A. compressed air-atomized burner firing light oil
    B. steam-atomized burner firing heavy oil
    C. air-atomized burner firing heavy oil
    D. mechanically-atomized burner firing heavy oil

17.____

18. It is usually desirable to have a program which will create and maintain the interest of workers in safety. Of the following, the one which such a program CANNOT do is to

    A. develop safe work habits
    B. compensate for unsafe procedures
    C. provide a channel of communications between workers and management
    D. give employees a chance to participate in accident prevention activities

18.____

19. Because of a ruptured ammonia tank, the concentration of ammonia gas in a room exceeds 3%.
    The wearing of a gas mask, as the only protective device, by a person entering the room is

    A. *recommended,* because the gas mask alone is sufficient protection
    B. *not recommended,* because the ammonia will severely irritate the skin
    C. *not recommended,* because the gas mask is not effective at concentrations above 3%
    D. *not recommended,* because ammonia is flammable

19.____

20. The Occupational Safety and Health Act of 1970 provided for

    A. penalties against employees for safety violations
    B. complete occupational safety against all hazards
    C. standards of employee discipline
    D. employees' right to review a copy of a safety citation against the employer

20.____

21. An aftercooler on a reciprocating air compressor is used PRIMARILY to

    A. increase compressor capacity
    B. improve compressor efficiency
    C. condense the moisture in the compressed air
    D. cool the lubricating oil

21.____

22. The one of the following tasks which is an example of preventive maintenance is

    A. replacing a leaking water pipe nipple
    B. cleaning the cup on a rotary cup burner
    C. cleaning a completely clogged oil strainer
    D. replacing a blown fuse

22.____

23. The four MAIN causes of failure of three-phase electric motors are

    A. dirt, friction, moisture, single-phasing
    B. friction, moisture, single-phasing, vibration
    C. dirt, moisture, single-phasing, vibration
    D. dirt, friction, moisture, vibration

23.____

24. The one of the following electrical control components that may be lubricated is the

   A. drum controller's copper-to-copper contacts
   B. relay bearing
   C. starter silver contact
   D. shunt spring

25. In the planning of a preventive maintenance program, the FIRST requirement is to

   A. prepare a maintenance manual
   B. inventory the equipment
   C. inventory the tools available
   D. prepare repair requisitions for all equipment not operating satisfactorily

## KEY (CORRECT ANSWERS)

| | | | |
|---|---|---|---|
| 1. | D | 11. | D |
| 2. | A | 12. | A |
| 3. | C | 13. | C |
| 4. | B | 14. | A |
| 5. | D | 15. | D |
| 6. | B | 16. | B |
| 7. | A | 17. | D |
| 8. | C | 18. | B |
| 9. | B | 19. | B |
| 10. | B | 20. | D |

| | |
|---|---|
| 21. | C |
| 22. | B |
| 23. | D |
| 24. | A |
| 25. | B |

# EXAMINATION SECTION
## TEST 1

DIRECTIONS: Each question or incomplete statement is followed by several suggested answers or completions. Select the one that BEST answers the question or completes the statement. *PRINT THE LETTER OF TEE CORRECT ANSWER IN THE SPACE AT THE RIGHT.*

1. As a stationary engineer with an operating department, you are asked to consider the factors which should be taken into account in the selection of a new steam generator. Of the following, the one which has the LEAST effect upon the selection of a new steam generator (boiler) is the

   A. type of fuel to be used
   B. pressure and temperature of steam required
   C. expected steam load variations
   D. type of electrical energy to be generated, i.e., AC or DC

2. Various authorities agree that *spalling* of the refractory lining in the furnace of a steam generator is said to exist when the *refractory cracks and breaks away at the surface*. A PRIMARY cause of spalling is

   A. uneven heating and cooling within the refractory brick
   B. continuous overfiring of the boiler
   C. slag accumulations on furnace walls
   D. change in fuel from solid to liquid type

3. For laying-up a boiler for prolonged out of service periods, the alternate to the *dry method* is the *wet method*.
   The wet method provides that after the boiler has been completely cleaned and checked, it be filled to the vent valve with deaerated water to which a solution of caustic soda and sodium sulphite has been added.
   The pH value of this fluid in the boiler should be controlled and maintained in the range of

   A. 1 to 4      B. 3 to 6      C. 6 to 11      D. 13 to 14

4. In a properly operated steam generator, the amount of blowdown is adjusted to some percentage of the steam flow, as approximated from tests, to keep the boiler-water solids concentration at or below some set limit.
   If we assume a limit of 850 ppm solids in boiler water, the 30% make up with 110 ppm solids, then for each 1000 lbs. of steam generated, the quantity of blowdown should be HOST NEARLY _____ ' lbs.

   A. 40      B. 60      C. 80      D. 100

5. A steam generator is to be laid up for a rather long period of time. Of the several methods recommended for laying-up the boiler, the dry method is to be used, with the unit closed tightly.
   In this method, the drums and mud boxes are sealed after first placing trays of _____ in them.

   A. hot zeolite           B. unslaked lime
   C. trisodium phosphate   D. calcium chloride

6. A given boiler is being fired in a proper manner for warm-up before being placed on the line. This boiler is one of a battery of four, all connected to the same header. This one boiler is equipped with a non-return valve.
The purpose of this non-return valve is to prevent the flow of

    A. steam from the boiler until boiler pressure is above the header pressure
    B. feedwater from the boiler until boiler pressure is above the feedwater main pressure
    C. air into the boiler as it is being warmed up
    D. steam through the gauge glass in the event it should break

6.___

7. The PRIME fundamentals for proper and complete combustion are

    A. temperature and properly heated refractory
    B. time, temperature, and turbulence
    C. turbulence and forced draft
    D. turbulence, forced and induced draft, properly heated refractory, and non-slagging fly ash

7.___

8. In a given boiler, the lump size of bituminous coal is to be hand fired.
Assuming that the grates have been properly designed and installed for firing this coal, the system of hand firing which should be used for MOST efficient combustion is the

    A. spreading method
    B. spreading method, along with occasional use of the alternate method
    C. alternate method, thereby doing away with the use of a slice bar
    D. coking method

8.___

9. The absorbing reagent which is used to absorb $CO_2$ is

    A. potassium pyrogallate
    B. cuprous chloride
    C. potassium hydroxide (caustic potash)
    D. hydrogen dioxide

9.___

10. The absorbing reagent which is used to absorb CO is

    A. hydrogen dioxide      B. potassium hydroxide
    C. potassium pyrogallate      D. cuprous chloride

10.___

11. The absorbing reagent which is used to absorb $O_2$ is

    A. potassium pyrogallate      B. potassium hydroxide
    C. cuprous chloride      D. hydrogen dioxide

11.___

12. Many factors are involved in the design of a furnace which should cover every possible operating condition.
A device which is commonly used to preserve and prolong the life of furnace walls where furnace temperatures are high due to overfiring is the

    A. ignition-arch      B. bridgewall
    C. water-wall      D. back-arch

12.___

13. A poor grade of anthracite coal is properly burned in a furnace. A complete analysis of the flue gas is made.
    The one constituent which is probably present in this flue gas and which is potentially MOST corrosive is

    A. $H_2O$    B. CO    C. $SO_2$    D. $CO_2$

    13.____

14. Many existing steam generators which are coal fired (both hand and mechanical) are equipped with a system of balanced draft.
    With this system operating properly, the over fire draft should be MOST NEARLY _____ " w.g.

    A. +1.02    B. -1.02    C. -0.00    D. -0.02

    14.____

15. An operating boiler is generating superheated steam at 200 #/sq. and total temperature of 420° F. The operating engineer notes that the flue gas temperature in the stack is close to 1000° F. This unit is equipped with both an economizer and an air preheater. Of the following, the one set of conditions which is MOST likely NOT responsible for the 1000° F flue gas temperature is

    A. improper operation of the soot blower
    B. broken baffles in the boiler
    C. overfiring the boiler at a high rate in the flue gas
    D. a very high percentage of $CO_2$

    15.____

16. The manner in which fuel oils are treated before firing depends greatly on their viscosity. The MOST widely accepted standard test method which may be used to determine the viscosity of the various grades of fuel oil is commonly known as the _____ Universal Viscosimeter.

    A. Saybolt    B. Kinematic    C. Absolute    D. Potential

    16.____

17. A particular boiler is fired by means of straight mechanical pressure type (no return flow) burners using number 6 oil.
    The operating pressure range of these burners is such that atomization and operating characteristics become unstable if the pressure at the base of the nozzle falls below _____ psi.

    A. 180    B. 120    C. 50    D. 80

    17.____

18. A particular boiler has been designed for firing a small size of anthracite coal on a traveling grate stoker. This boiler furnace is provided with the new type rear arches.
    If we assume that moderately high grate speeds (approximately 40'/hr.) can be used, then the combustion rates can be anywhere from _____ lbs./sq.ft./hr.

    A. 5 to 10    B. 15 to 20    C. 30 to 40    D. 60 to 100

    18.____

19. With regard to the purchase of fuel oils, the *degree API at 60° F* is generally always given in the specification. With regard to this factor, one can always say that the calorific value in BTU gal will

    A. increase as the degree API at 60° F increases
    B. decrease as the degree API at 60° F increases

    19.____

C. not be affected by changes in the degree API at 60° F
D. increase as the degree API at 60° F rises to 25 and thereafter decrease

20. A recent development in the mechanical straight pressure type burner design is the use of a double tube gun. One tube is used to feed oil to the tip, and the other provides a passage for the unused oil to be returned.
In operation, with number 6 fuel oil, the important advantage of this design is that it

  A. gives good atomization with a wide variation in capacity
  B. permits the use of the flat flame as opposed to the hollow conical flame
  C. permits the use of a fuel oil piping system with both high and low suction lines
  D. allows the operator to fire fuel oil efficiently at reasonably low temperatures (approximately 120° F)

21. In order to fire fuel oil efficiently, it must be properly atomized immediately before it is mixed with the combustion air.
The type of fuel oil burner which is generally considered MOST costly to operate is a _____ atomizing burner.

  A. high-pressure air  B. steam
  C. low-pressure air   D. mechanical

22. Gasket materials, for use in making up pipe flanges, must be made of materials which will not be chemically or thermally affected by the fluid in the pipe.
Gaskets made of red rubber are MOST generally used for _____ for temperatures up to _____° F.

  A. oil; 200           B. steam or water; 600
  C. water; 700         D. air; 200

23. Gaskets made of corrugated copper are MOST generally used for _____ for temperatures up to _____° F.

  A. steam; 600         B. steam or water; 1000
  C. oil; 1000          D. steam, water, or oil; 1000

24. An industrial heating process in a given plant uses bled steam at 30 psi. Accurate and close temperature control is required for this process, and it is considered necessary that the steam trap used to drain condensate be of the continuously operating type.
Therefore, the type of steam trap which most definitely should NOT be used is the

  A. combination float and thermostatic
  B. thermostatic
  C. combination inverted bucket and thermostatic
  D. ball float with external thermostatic element

25. A deaerating type feedwater heater is now considered an essential piece of equipment in steam-electric generating stations. This is especially so if the generated steam pressures are comparatively high. This type of feedwater heater removes non-condensible gas such as air, free oxygen, carbon dioxide, etc.
    If these are permitted to remain in the feedwater, they tend to

    A. gum up the feedwater strainers and pump valves
    B. increase scale formation and corrosion in the boilers
    C. increase *surging* in the boiler and *blistering* in the tubes
    D. destroy the lead metallic gaskets used in the pipe flanges

25.____

---

# KEY (CORRECT ANSWERS)

1. D
2. C
3. D
4. A
5. B

6. A
7. B
8. D
9. C
10. D

11. B
12. C
13. C
14. D
15. D

16. A
17. C
18. D
19. A
20. A

21. A
22. D
23. A
24. D
25. B

---

# TEST 2

DIRECTIONS: Each question or incomplete statement is followed by several suggested answers or completions. Select the one that BEST answers the question or completes the statement. *PRINT THE LETTER OF THE CORRECT ANSWER IN THE SPACE AT THE RIGHT.*

1. For a given plant, you are preparing to purchase valve seats and disks for the overhaul of the water end of a duplex direct-acting steam driven boiler feedwater pump. The material of which the valve disks should be made for this service is

    A. hard moulded rubber  
    B. neoprene  
    C. machined cast iron  
    D. bronze

    1.____

2. Several types of duplex direct-acting steam driven pumps are in use for feedwater service in many steam generating plants. A basic difference relates to the use of the piston type and the outside packed plunger type pumps. From the point of view of the operating and maintenance personnel, in a given plant, the outside packed plunger type is considered more desirable.
   This opinion is acceptable because

    A. this type of pump is heavier and therefore more enduring
    B. for equal capacity, considerably less steam is used
    C. all packing leakage is external and is a guide for making adjustments
    D. plunger and packing friction is greatly reduced

    2.____

3. Pumps of the centrifugal type are generally manufactured in one of two general patterns, i.e., turbine with a diffuser ring, or volute without a diffuser ring. In the volute pattern pumps, the discharger chamber acts as a diffuser.
   The PRIMARY purpose of a diffuser ring or chamber is to

    A. convert high velocity to pressure
    B. convert high pressure to velocity
    C. convert the end thrust to a balanced side thrust
    D. bring about a balanced end thrust condition

    3.____

4. The recommended procedure for starting a turbine type centrifugal pump handling 100°F water which has a submerged suction is

    A. prime pump, start pump motor, open discharge valve, and then open suction valve
    B. open suction valve, start pump motor, when pump is up to speed gradually open the discharge valve
    C. open discharge valve, start pump motor, when pump is up to speed gradually open suction valve
    D. open discharge valve, start pump motor, prime pump, and then open suction valve gradually

    4.____

5. Some steam generating plants are equipped with injectors as standby equipment for their duplex direct-acting steam pumps. Assume that these injectors are of the single-tube lifting type.
   When one of these injectors is placed in operation, the steam will FIRST enter a(n)

    5.____

A. suction tube
B. combining tube
C. expanding nozzle
D. delivery tube

6. A duplex direct-acting steam driven pump with outside packed plungers is being put back in operation after being completely overhauled. As part of the overhaul work, the steam valves were replaced and set up with greatly reduced lost motion.
   When this pump is started, the probability is that it will operate

   A. at greatly reduced speed
   B. at somewhat increased speed
   C. with a short stroke
   D. with a long stroke

7. Upon receiving a shipment of thermometers, you find that all of the instruments are calibrated with the centigrade instead of the fahrenheit scale.
   If you had to use one of these thermometers to determine the temperature of boiler feedwater, then a reading of 55° centigrade would be equal to _____ °fahrenheit.

   A. 131    B. 99    C. 138.6    D. 62.5

8. The water end of a duplex direct-acting steam driven plunger type boiler feedwater pump (double acting) has a bore of 3" and a stroke of 6". During the course of a one-hour test run, the speed is maintained constant at 50 rpm. Test data as follows is recorded:

   | | |
   |---|---|
   | Average water temperature | = 160° F |
   | Total weight of water pumped | = 16200# |
   | Specific gravity 160° F | = 0.98 |
   | Weight of a gallon of water 160° F | = 8.16# |
   | Volume of one U.S. gallon | = 231 cu.in. |

   Under the above conditions, the slip in this pump is MOST NEARLY _____ %.

   A. 10    B. 5    C. 3    D. 1/2

Questions 9-10.

DIRECTIONS: Questions 9 and 10 are to be answered on the basis of the following information.

The name plate data on a water tube boiler gives, in addition to the manufacturer's name, address, shop, and serial number, the following information:

| | |
|---|---|
| Number of 4" tubes: | - 60 |
| Number of 2" tubes: | - 150 |
| Length of tubes: | - 25' |

Other data, such as total tube heating surface, boiler horsepower, etc. are so worn as to be unreadable. In operation, the boiler generates saturated steam at 125 psi. (The total heat required to generate a pound of steam under operating conditions is 1040 BTU/#.)

9. Disregarding drums, the total square footage of generating surface is MOST NEARLY

   A. 41,000    B. 18,100    C. 9,100    D. 3,500

10. Assume that the average heat transfer rate through the total tube surface is 3000 BTU sq.ft./hr. when operating at full load.
    Under these conditions, the hourly steam generating rate becomes MOST NEARLY _____ #/hr.

    A. 26300   B. 10200   C. 52400   D. 118400

11. For a given ventilating system in a building, it is desired that the c.f.m. handled by the fan in the system be increased by 50%, i.e., from 8000 c.f.m. to 12000 c.f.m. The fan is motor driven by means of a v-belt drive. The present fan speed is 450 rpm.
    In order to increase the fan output as given above, the new fan speed should be MOST NEARLY _____ rpm.

    A. 1010   B. 875   C. 750   D. 675

12. The following operating conditions exist for a given boiler:
    Steam pressure — 125#/sq.in. gauge
    Steam temperature (assume steam is delivered saturated and dry) — 353° F
    Feedwater temperature — 190° F
    Total heat of steam as delivered (enthalpy) — 1193 BTU/#
    Heat of liquid at 190° F — 158 BTU/#
    Calorific value of coal as fired — 13000 BTU/#

    As the result of the most recent test, the overall boiler efficiency is to be taken as 71%. In keeping with the above data, we may expect that for each pound of coal fired, the pounds of steam generated will be MOST NEARLY

    A. 10.91   B. 12.55   C. 8.91   D. 6.81

13. A given boiler, in operation, generates 50,000 # Hr. of steam at 200 #/sq.in. gauge, total temperature of 440° F, and total heat (enthalpy) of 1234.0. Feedwater is delivered to this boiler at a temperature of 190° F, and the heat of the liquid at this temperature is 158 BTU/#. The latent heat of vaporization for water at atmospheric pressure and 212° F is 970.3 BTU/#.
    For the above outlined operating conditions, the Factor of Evaporation is MOST NEARLY

    A. 1.11   B. 1.27   C. 1.43   D. 0.903

14. After a good indicator card has been taken for a steam engine, the following equation is used to figure the Indicated Horsepower:

    $$I.H.P = \frac{PLAN}{K}$$

    When N is given in rpm, then the numerical value of the constant K in the above equation is USUALLY equal to

    A. 5250   B. 33000   C. 1728   D. 550

15. A simplex double acting, horizontal, reciprocating steam engine is equipped with corliss type valve gear. This valve gear is of the releasing type.
    In order to get a sharp cut-off, _____ must be used.

A. a 600-w lubricant, to keep the valve gear free,
B. properly adjusted dashpots
C. a centrifugal inertia type governor
D. a single eccentric for control of all four valves

16. If a copper coil is rotated in a clockwise direction at a uniform speed in a uniform magnetic field, the induced voltage in the coil will be alternating in direction.
    To obtain direct current from this coil when connected to an external circuit, it is common practice to use

    A. two slip rings
    B. one slip ring
    C. a commutator
    D. a balancer coil

17. Electrical apparatus such as a motor or generator which has been idle for some time in a damp location may have accumulated moisture and is, therefore, unsafe to put into operation. The apparatus should be dried out thoroughly before being returned to service and periodic insulation resistance measurements taken while in the process of drying out. This is done by using a(n)

    A. growler
    B. ammeter
    C. wattmeter
    D. megger

18. In reference to a dynamo, brush holders are used to guide and eliminate vibration of brushes, which is a common cause of sparking. The brushes are held against the commutator surface by adjustable springs.
    For BEST operation, the spring tension should be adjusted so that brushes press against the commutator with a force of _____ lbs. per sq. in.

    A. 1.5 to 2.0
    B. 0.5 to 1.0
    C. 2.75 to 3.50
    D. 3.75 to 4.50

19. A power plant uses direct current generators to deliver electrical energy to a 3 wire balanced system of distribution.
    Assuming that two (2) balance coils are used but are placed outside of the generator, then connection to the armature winding is USUALLY made through _____ slip ring(s).

    A. 2
    B. 4
    C. 1
    D. 3

20. A steam engine is equipped with a flyball governor which is belt driven from a *driving* pulley mounted concentric with the engine shaft. This belt gives motion to a *receiving* pulley which is mounted on a stub shaft which, through bevel gears, gives motion to the governor shaft. Other things remaining the same, if the diameter of the receiving pulley is reduced, this engine would then MOST likely operate

    A. at a comparatively higher speed
    B. at the speed which existed before
    C. with a reduced cut-off
    D. at a comparatively lower speed

21. A nine stage impulse turbine is one in which the stationary vanes between the stages act to _____ the steam.

    A. reheat
    B. redirect
    C. re-expand
    D. recompress

22. A *rateau* or velocity stage is very often made part of a multi-stage impulse turbine. With respect to a nine stage impulse turbine, the velocity stage is GENERALLY the _____ stage.

 A. third B. ninth C. first D. fifth

23. You are asked to assist in setting up and taking indicator cards for a corliss type steam engine. The steam line pressure is 200 psi, and the overall pencil rise of the indicator is 2 1/2".
 The BEST *scale of the indicator spring* which should be used, if the allowable pencil rise is limited to 2", is MOST NEARLY

 A. 40 B. 50 C. 100 D. 200

24. The design of a particular turbine is such that the critical speed is above the operating speed. Assume that you are assigned to place this turbine in operation. After warming up both the steam header and turbine, you slowly begin to bring the unit up to rated speed (3600 rpm). At approximately 1400 rpm, the turbine rotor begins to vibrate severely.
 As the operator, you should

 A. increase the speed rapidly and re-open the turbine drains
 B. check the overspeed trip to make sure no one has tampered with it
 C. check the lube oil pressure to make sure it is sufficiently high
 D. decrease the speed quickly and recheck drains, lube oil, and warm-up procedure

25. A steam engine having two cylinders side by side with the high-pressure cylinder exhausting into the low-pressure cylinder is an engine which is

 A. tandem-compound B. cross-compound
 C. double D. duplex

## KEY (CORRECT ANSWERS)

| | |
|---|---|
| 1. A | 11. D |
| 2. C | 12. C |
| 3. A | 13. A |
| 4. B | 14. B |
| 5. A | 15. B |
| 6. C | 16. C |
| 7. A | 17. D |
| 8. A | 18. A |
| 9. D | 19. A |
| 10. B | 20. D |

21. B
22. D
23. C
24. D
25. B

# TEST 3

DIRECTIONS: Each question or incomplete statement is followed by several suggested answers or completions. Select the one that BEST answers the question or completes the statement. *PRINT THE LETTER OF THE CORRECT ANSWER IN THE SPACE AT THE RIGHT.*

1. A steam generator is supplied with two safety valves on the boiler drum and one on the superheater section.
   The superheater safety valve would be relieved

   A. at the same pressure as those on the drum
   B. at a pressure higher than those on the drum
   C. at a pressure lower than those on the drum
   D. by a predetermined temperature element device

2. The MAXIMUM size of blowdown piping for a boiler operating at 100 psi is _____ inch(es).

   A. 1     B. 1 1/2     C. 2 1/2     D. 4

3. Superheater steam CANNOT be generated in a boiler due to

   A. inadequate heat in the fuel
   B. the presence of saturated water
   C. lifting of safety valves
   D. impurities in the water

4. Which statement is MOST NEARLY correct?

   A. If a failure occurs in a water-tube boiler, it is less liable to explosion than a failure in a fire-tube boiler.
   B. It is safe to run a boiler at a higher pressure than that approved by the inspector.
   C. A dirty tube boiler produces steam as efficiently as a clean tube boiler.
   D. A boiler will operate efficiently with 1% CO.

5. The Hartford loop is USUALLY used on a

   A. heating boiler           B. high pressure boiler
   C. refrigeration unit       D. compressor

6. A fire-tube boiler, as compared to a water-tube boiler,

   A. is a faster steamer
   B. has a slower circulation rate
   C. is more economical
   D. can be made for high generation capacity rates

7. On a B & W cross drum inclined water-tube boiler, sinuous or serpentine headers are used to

   A. provide greater strength in header with stays
   B. give better appearance
   C. allow for staggering the tubes in relation to each other
   D. allow for easier cleaning of soot from tubes

8. Both ends of the straight tubes used in water-tube boilers are now customarily terminated in

    A. cylindrical drums with closed ends
    B. box headers
    C. sectional headers
    D. the steam drum

9. What would you use on an outside hand hole fitting on a sectional header of a cross drum water-tube boiler?
   A _____ gasket.

    A. raised lapped joint without a
    B. live thin rubber
    C. thin asbestos
    D. thin woven cotton

10. What is done BEFORE a hydrostatic test?

    A. Build a small fire in the boiler.
    B. Gag and clamp safety valves.
    C. Remove the water column.
    D. Increase the spring tension on safety valves.

11. On a 2" pop type safety valve set to blow at 280 psig, what is MOST NEARLY the total force, in lbs., on the seat of the valve at the time it starts to lift?

    A. 1100    B. 1000    C. 900    D. 600

12. The force required to lift a 3" safety valve with a pressure of 280 psi is _____ lbs.

    A. 840    B. 1979    C. 2520    D. 1680

13. A lever type safety valve has a 3" power arm, 4" diameter seat, and 24" weight arm. The weight necessary to allow the valve to lift at 50 psi is MOST NEARLY _____ lbs.

    A. 50    B. 60    C. 70    D. 80

14. In the sizing of anthracite coal, _____ is larger than _____ .

    A. nut; egg
    B. buckwheat no. 1; buckwheat no. 3
    C. stove; broken
    D. rice; pea

15. The size of anthracite coal which is between nut (chest- nut) and buckwheat #1 is known commercially as

    A. stove    B. pea    C. rice    D. barley

16. The MAXIMUM size opening in grate bars which should be used when burning pea coal is _____ inch.

    A. 3/4    B. 3/8    C. 5/8    D. 1/2

17. Buckwheat #3 coal is commercially known as

   A. rice
   B. pea
   C. nonpareil
   D. barley

18. On high pressure boilers, the water column is used in order to

   A. show directly to the operator the level of the water in the tubes
   B. find easily the pressure within the boiler
   C. dampen the oscillation of the water in the gauge glass
   D. prevent the boiler from exploding

19. Every power boiler must be provided with a steam gauge connected to the boiler steam space or to an intervening water column.
    The following equipment must be installed IMMEDIATELY before the gauge:

   A. Cock having a *T* or lever handle which is parallel to the connecting pipe when the cock is open
   B. Syphon to prevent the entrance of steam to the gauge
   C. 1/4 inch valved connection for attaching a test gauge when the boiler is operating
   D. all of the above

20. Why is a loop used on a steam gauge having a Bourdon tube?
    To

   A. allow for expansion and contraction
   B. stop fluctuation of steam pressure
   C. prevent hot steam from damaging the Bourdon tube
   D. prevent a slug of water from injuring the tube

21. Of the chemicals used in boiler water treatment, the one associated with oxygen removal is

   A. trisodium phosphate
   B. potassium chromate
   C. sodium sulphite
   D. magnesium sulphate

22. Organic compounds such as *tannins* and *quebracho* are often used in boiler water compounds containing soda ash or sodium phosphates.
    The purpose of the organic compounds is to

   A. reduce hydrolysis of softening chemicals
   B. disperse sludge formed by softening chemicals so they do not stick to heating surfaces
   C. soften water and remove oxygen
   D. form sludges and increase alkalinity

23. The chemical often used in boiler water treatment to coagulate and settle out solids in the boiler water, so that they may be removed by blowdown, is

   A. sodium aluminate
   B. aluminum sulphate
   C. iron phosphate
   D. sodium silicate

24. The Schneider method of determining the alkalinity concentration in boiler water consists of  24.___

    A. mechanical reproduction of the boiler water condition
    B. an electric method of measuring the conductivity
    C. a direct reading chemical determination by titration and neutralization
    D. utilization of improved methods of adding pyrites

25. Excessive amounts of boiler compound will lead to  25.___

    A. corrosion                         B. pitting
    C. caustic embrittlement       D. lower steam temperature

---

## KEY (CORRECT ANSWERS)

| | | | |
|---|---|---|---|
| 1. | C | 11. | C |
| 2. | C | 12. | B |
| 3. | B | 13. | D |
| 4. | A | 14. | B |
| 5. | A | 15. | B |
| 6. | B | 16. | D |
| 7. | C | 17. | D |
| 8. | C | 18. | A |
| 9. | D | 19. | D |
| 10. | B | 20. | C |

| | |
|---|---|
| 21. | C |
| 22. | B |
| 23. | A |
| 24. | C |
| 25. | C |

---

# EXAMINATION SECTION
# TEST 1

DIRECTIONS: Each question or incomplete statement is followed by several suggested answers or completions. Select the one that BEST answers the question or completes the statement. *PRINT THE LETTER OF THE CORRECT ANSWER IN THE SPACE AT THE RIGHT.*

1. Before a newly installed boiler is placed in operation, it is recommended that it be *boiled out* for a period ranging from 36 to 72 hours. A suggested method is to use soda ash and caustic soda.
   If a steam boiler operator were to use this method, then for each 1000 lbs. of water which the boiler holds at the steaming level, he should use MOST NEARLY _____ lbs. of soda ash and _____ lbs. of caustic soda.

   A. 10; 10    B. 5; 10    C. 9; 9    D. 3; 3

   1.____

2. With regard to fire-tube boilers, the letters H.R.T. MOST likely mean

   A. highly regulated temperature
   B. highly regulated thermostat
   C. horizontal return tubular
   D. horizontal rotated tubes

   2.____

3. Baffles are generally arranged in water tube boilers to control and direct the flow of flue gas. In a given boiler, the baffles are arranged to direct the flow of flue gas essentially parallel to the tube length.
   This is commonly referred to as _____ baffling.

   A. cross            B. vertical
   C. angle            D. longitudinal

   3.____

4. Straight water tubes are sometimes constructed with front and rear *box headers*. The front box headers may be riveted directly to the steam drum, and hand holes are provided to allow tube inspection, cleaning, and replacement.
   Stay bolts are provided and connect the plate and tube sheet in order to prevent

   A. bulging under internal pressure
   B. blistering due to internal heat
   C. collapsing under internal vacuum
   D. bagging under internal weight

   4.____

5. Straight inclined water tube boilers may be constructed in two general designs, i.e., longitudinal drum arrangement or cross drum arrangement.
   A feature of cross drum arrangement is that this type of construction GENERALLY results in a

   A. loss of head room
   B. saving of head room
   C. loss of combustion or furnace volume
   D. loss of economy for large capacities

   5.____

6. A boiler which has been in operation for approximately one (1) year without any *outage* period is to be taken off the line for internal inspection. (This boiler is one of five in a battery with the other four remaining in operation.) This one boiler has to be properly cooled and emptied.
Before any man is permitted to enter the drum, the CORRECT safety procedure requires that

   A. he be equipped with safety light and clothing
   B. he be provided with a safety line
   C. the drum be ventilated and the safety valve be gagged
   D. the main steam, blowdown, and feedwater *stops* be closed, chained, and tagged

7. In keeping with the most recent local law, a high pressure steam boiler is one which has a capacity of more than ten horsepower to generate steam and carries a pressure of MORE than _____ psi.

   A. 10     B. 15     C. 25     D. 75

8. In a particular plant, all the boilers have straight inclined water tubes rolled into sectional headers of serpentine design. The tubes in the upper bank are all 1" in diameter, and those in the lower bank are all 4" in diameter.
In these boilers, the hand holes for the upper tube banks (all hand holes of same size) would MOST likely permit easy access to _____ tubes.

   A. individual
   B. super heater
   C. economizer
   D. a group of

9. In a particular plant, all of the steam boilers are of the Stirling type.
In order to maintain the outside surface of the tubes in the boiler in good condition, an operator should use

   A. the hot-lime water treatment procedure
   B. the zeolite system of water treatment
   C. soot blowers, such as diamond or equal
   D. a combination of induced and forced draft

10. In a given plant, the boilers are of the locomotive type. In order to maintain the outside surface of the tubes in good condition while the boiler is in operation, an operator should use

    A. recommended feedwater treatment as directed
    B. diamond soot blowers of the rotating impulse type
    C. diamond soot blowers of the telescope retraction type
    D. periodic surface blows

11. Several of the vertical fire tube boilers are so designed that the tubes extend above the operating water level.
In the continuous and prolonged operation of a boiler of this design at rated load, a POSSIBLE result would be

    A. an expanded lower tube sheet
    B. repeated burning out of the fusible plug
    C. generation of steam with a very high degree of super heat
    D. leaks at the upper tube sheet due to possible tube overheating

12. The economizer is the device by means of which feedwater temperature is raised by heat recovery from the flue gas. From a thermal point of view, the use of an economizer increases the steam-generator efficiency.
    The results of tests show that for each 10° to 11° F increase in feedwater temperature, the efficiency increases APPROXIMATELY _____ %.

    A. 1  B. 5  C. 7.5  D. 3.5

    12._____

13. Which one of the following statements is CORRECT?

    A. A *pendant* type superheater is always self-draining.
    B. The *overdeck* convection type superheater with two headers, both set below the tube elements, is always self-draining.
    C. In a radiant type superheater, the final steam temperature tends to rise as the load increases.
    D. In a convection type superheater, the final steam temperature tends to fall as the load increases.

    13._____

14. Riveted joints in boiler drums and sheets must be made in accordance with the local code.
    A triple-riveted butt joint with unequal straps, if used, must have a TOTAL of _____ rows of rivets.

    A. six  B. nine  C. three  D. five

    14._____

15. The design of a steam generator (boiler) is directed toward the final erection and operation of the unit as a step in the use of heat in the conversion of energy from one form to another.
    The operation of the steam generator (boiler) should be carried on in such manner as to assure, as a PRIMARY consideration, the

    A. conservation of fuel
    B. conservation of materials
    C. reduction of risks to personnel
    D. reduction of waste in the use of steam

    15._____

16. An operating steam generator is equipped with three safety valves which are numbered and located as follows: #D-1 on the boiler steam drum, #D-2 on the boiler steam drum, and #S-1 on outlet header of the superheater.
    These safety valves should be set so that

    A. all three blow at the same pressure
    B. number S-1 blows first
    C. number D-1 blows first
    D. numbers D-1 and D-2 blow at the same pressure ahead of number S-1

    16._____

Questions 17-18.

DIRECTIONS: Questions 17 and 18 are to be answered on the basis of the following information.

A given boiler is of the bent-tube type, with the drum axis parallel to the long axis of the furnace. The design is such that the upper drum is twice the length of the mud drum, and has front, half length side headers to provide for a water-cooled furnace. Feedwater enters the rear of the mud drum and is directed from there through tubes in the last convection pass to the upper drum. A bridge wall is set across the furnace directly in front of the mud drum.

17. This arrangement for feedwater travel is

    A. desirable because an economizer action is thus developed
    B. desirable because one less connection is made into the upper drum, giving a higher ligament coefficient
    C. desirable because cooler flue gas eliminates the need for induced draft fans
    D. not desirable because relatively cool water is being directed through tubes across which flow the hottest flue gases

18. In this boiler, the boiler tubes, with respect to size, are arranged as follows: larger tubes in the water walls and first two passes; smaller tubes, properly nested, in the last pass, arranged with baffles to give cross flow. This arrangement of smaller tubes and cross baffles in the last pass is DESIRABLE (although draft loss is increased) because it

    A. gives greater heat absorbing area
    B. is easier to handle and repair smaller diameter tubes
    C. gives better support to the cross baffles
    D. gives lower internal friction loss (fluid flow)

19. Fundamentally, water-tube boilers fall into two groups, i.e., straight tube type, or bent tube type.
    The particular advantage, from a maintenance point of view, which favors the straight tube type is that

    A. hanging baffles are more readily supported
    B. individual tubes are more readily replaced
    C. by-pass dampers are more accessible
    D. dusting and access doors may be set on any one of three sides

20. A straight water tube type boiler has been baffled in such a manner as to hold a relatively constant flue gas velocity through the several passes.
    Under this condition, it can be said that the cross-sectional area of the

    A. first pass is less than that of the second or third pass
    B. second pass is less than that of the first or third pass
    C. third pass is less than that of the first or second pass
    D. three passes are equal to one another

21. A given boiler is to be taken *off the line* for annual inspection and repairs.
    In keeping with a good suggested shut down procedure, the boiler may be EMPTIED (drained) when

    A. the setting is cool enough to permit entry into the furnace
    B. the boiler water temperature has dropped to approximately 180° F
    C. the pressure has fallen to approximately half of the operating pressure
    D. 48 hours have elapsed after killing the fires

22. In most power plants, the accepted procedure is to blow down the boilers at least once every 24 hours (when blow down is not continuous or controlled by analysis of the boiler water).
The BEST time for this single blow down is when the steamrate is at

    A. 80% of capacity
    B. 125% of capacity
    C. 50% of capacity
    D. its lowest point

23. Practically all boilers are equipped in such a manner that the gauge glass and water column are provided with blow down valves.
In MOST plants, the operating rules provide that the water column and gauge glass be blown down

    A. not more than once each two watches (8 hour watches) in underfired plants
    B. at least once each watch (8 hour watch)
    C. at least once each day (24 hours)
    D. whenever the engineer on watch thinks of doing so

24. A given boiler, equipped with a superheater, is being placed *on the line* to operate along with a battery of other boilers (200 psi and 100° F superheat).
In accepted operating procedure, the drains on the superheater outlet header should remain OPEN untilboiler pressure reaches _____ psi.

    A. 25    B. 50    C. 180    D. 5

25. On a boiler having the gauge glass and water column blow downs entering the ash pit, the fireman does not close the blowdown valve all the way; the valve remains cracked.
The MOST immediate effect is a

    A. decrease in boiler efficiency
    B. false level in water glass; that is, gauge will show water too low
    C. sharp drop in draft pressure in ash pit
    D. drop in boiler capacity

## KEY (CORRECT ANSWERS)

| | | | |
|---|---|---|---|
| 1. | D | 11. | D |
| 2. | C | 12. | A |
| 3. | D | 13. | B |
| 4. | A | 14. | A |
| 5. | B | 15. | C |
| 6. | D | 16. | B |
| 7. | B | 17. | A |
| 8. | D | 18. | A |
| 9. | C | 19. | B |
| 10. | A | 20. | C |

21. A
22. D
23. B
24. C
25. B

# TEST 2

DIRECTIONS: Each question or incomplete statement is followed by several suggested answers or completions. Select the one that BEST answers the question or completes the statement. *PRINT THE LETTER OF THE CORRECT ANSWER IN THE SPACE AT THE RIGHT.*

1. The type of furnace forming a boxlike extension enclosing the front section or all of the grate, often used to burn highly volatile fuels or fuels with high moisture content such as sawdust, bagasse, and refuse, is known as a(n)

    A. integral furnace
    B. ignition arch
    C. kiln
    D. Dutch oven

    1.____

2. The quantity of overfire air or secondary air used in chain grate stokers, expressed as a percentage of total air needed for combustion, is MOST NEARLY

    A. 5 to 10   B. 10 to 15   C. 15 to 20   D. 20 to 25

    2.____

3. If the drum safety valves on a boiler are set at 150 lbs., in no case shall the dial of the steam gauge be graduated to less than _____ lbs.

    A. 200   B. 225   C. 250   D. 275

    3.____

4. A waste heat boiler has more than 500 square feet of water heating surface, its safety valves are set to blow at 20 lbs., and it is equipped with 1 boiler feed pump.
   There must be the following additional equipment for feeding water to the boiler:

    A. A second boiler feed pump
    B. An injector
    C. An inspirator
    D. No additional equipment is required

    4.____

5. You are an engineer in a new plant.
   What would you consider MOST necessary on a battery of boilers?

    A. Automatic damper regulator
    B. Injector
    C. Feed pump
    D. Steam traps

    5.____

6. With regard to safety valves, when preparing for a hydrostatic test, you should

    A. screw down the compression screw on top of the spring
    B. set the safety at maximum working pressure
    C. set the safety at 150% of rating
    D. remove the valve or hold it down with a clamp

    6.____

7. A rotary cup oil burner can be distinguished because it has a(n)

    A. oil line and centrifugal fan
    B. oil line and steam line
    C. oil line and compressed air line
    D. steam line and two compressed air lines

    7.____

8. Regarding caustic embrittlement, it can be correctly said that when this condition exists in an H.P. steam boiler, it is USUALLY

   A. found at riveted drum seams
   B. caused by wet steam
   C. caused by too much scale on the tubes
   D. due to boiler corrosion

9. Boiler feed water treatment is usually undertaken in a boiler which exceeds 125 lbs. pressure.
   This is done to REDUCE

   A. the need for blowdown
   B. sludge in the mud drum
   C. sludge in the steam drum
   D. hard scale on the tubes

10. Atomization of fuel oil in a horizontal rotary cup burner is PRIMARILY due to the

    A. rotating cup *only*
    B. whirling action of the secondary air
    C. rotating cup and primary air
    D. pressure of the oil

11. Which of the following statements is MOST NEARLY correct?

    A. The shape of the fire on a horizontal rotary burner can be controlled by the shape of the cup.
    B. The cup on a horizontal rotary burner rotates at 800 rpm.
    C. A horizontal rotary cup burner needs no blower.
    D. With a horizontal rotary cup burner, the oil does not need to be heated.

12. One of the MAJOR advantages of the horizontal rotary burner is that

    A. the shape of the fire can be controlled by the shape of the cup
    B. there are comparatively few moving parts
    C. the air nozzle never needs to be cleaned
    D. the air nozzle controls both the primary and secondary air

13. The speed, in rpm, of the cup of a motor-driven horizontal rotary type oil burner is MOST NEARLY

    A. 1200     B. 1800     C. 2400     D. 3450

14. On a rotary cup oil burner using No. 6 fuel oil, the PRIMARY air is approximately _____%.

    A. 5     B. 25     C. 50     D. 70

15. Operating the horizontal rotary burner under normal conditions, the air nozzle causes the fire to commence from the atomizing cup, a distance MOST NEARLY

    A. right at the edge of the cup     B. 1/2 inch
    C. 1 inch                           D. several inches

16. If the flame on a horizontal rotary burner is reduced so low that it begins to break away from the cup and this cannot be overcome by closing the primary air damper, then the _____ should be _____.

    A. air nozzle size; increased
    B. air nozzle size; reduced
    C. secondary air damper; opened
    D. fuel oil pressure; reduced

17. The proper mixture of coal dust and air that should be maintained INSIDE of a coal pulverizer is _____% of total air required for combustion.

    A. 15 to 25    B. 25 to 35    C. 35 to 45    D. 45 to 55

18. The proper mixture of coal dust and air that should be maintained in a coal pulverizer is a(n)

    A. rich mixture
    B. lean mixture
    C. correct mixture to support combustion
    D. equal mixture of coal and air

19. What would you consider GOOD combustion?

    A. 12% $CO_2$ and 2% CO
    B. 12% $CO_2$ and 0% CO
    C. 14% $CO_2$ and 4% CO
    D. 7% $CO_2$ and 3% $O_2$

20. The use of water walls in modern steam boilers is to

    A. increase furnace volume
    B. increase the amount of refractory
    C. reduce the amount of refractory and increase the heating surface
    D. decrease excess air requirements

21. In insulating an H.P. boiler, you would use

    A. fire brick, which is shorter than building brick
    B. building brick
    C. fire clay
    D. refractory material

22. Regarding a pulverized coal boiler, which statement is NOT correct?

    A. A lower excess air can be carried.
    B. There is no slag on the first rows of tubes.
    C. There is excessive fly ash.
    D. The pulverized coal is not likely to contain excessive moisture.

23. Baffles are used in a boiler 23.___

    A. along the tubes *only*
    B. across the tubes *only*
    C. along and/or across the tubes
    D. to reflect heat

24. How many baffles are there in a 3-pass B & W boiler? 24.___

    A. 1  B. 2  C. 3  D. 4

25. In a longitudinal drum water-tube boiler, the superheater is GENERALLY placed 25.___

    A. in the first pass
    B. between the first and second passes
    C. in the third pass
    D. in the breeching

---

# KEY (CORRECT ANSWERS)

1. B 11. A
2. B 12. A
3. B 13. D
4. D 14. B
5. C 15. A

6. D 16. D
7. A 17. B
8. A 18. A
9. D 19. B
10. C 20. C

21. D
22. B
23. C
24. B
25. A

# EXAMINATION SECTION
# TEST 1

DIRECTIONS: Each question or incomplete statement is followed by several suggested answers or completions. Select the one that BEST answers the question or completes the statement. *PRINT THE LETTER OF THE CORRECT ANSWER IN THE SPACE AT THE RIGHT.*

1. What is the safe working pressure, in pounds, of a boiler with a 5/8 inch plate, 60,000 lb. tensile strength,
   60 inch diameter and triple riveted joints, using a factor of safety of 5?

   (Use the formula: Safe working pressure = $\frac{2 \times S \times T \times E}{F \times T}$)

   A. 115  
   B. 185.5  
   C. 217.5  
   D. None of the above

   1.____

2. What is the mechanical efficiency of an engine which delivers 200 brake H.P. while showing 250 indicated H.P.?

   (Use the formula: Mechanical efficiency = $\frac{\text{Brake H.P.}}{\text{Indicated H.P.}}$)

   A. 80%   B. 90%   C. 95%   D. 100%

   2.____

3. A pump delivers 500 cubic feet of water per minute and the pump displacement is 560 cubic feet. What is the slip?

   (Use the formula: Slip = $\frac{\text{Displacement - Volumn}}{\text{Displacement}}$)

   A. 10.7%   B. 15.5%   C. 18.7%   D. 21.3%

   3.____

4. A boiler is operating under 120 psi absolute pressure with feedwater at 160°F. The factor of evaporation is 1.063.5/970.4 = 1.097.
   If the total evaporation is 8,760 lb/hr., what boiler horsepower is the boiler developing?
   (Use the formula:

   Boiler H.P. = $\frac{\text{Total Evaporation} \times \text{Factor of Evaporation}}{34.5}$)

   A. 300   B. 278   C. 236   D. 212

   4.____

5. If an ammonia system was working at 15 lb. gage suction pressure and the temperature of liquid ammonia entering the evaporator through the expansion valve was 90°F., how many BTU per lb. would be available for useful work, assuming that the total heat of 1 lb. of ammonia at
   15 lb. gage pressure is 611.4 BTU and the heat of the liquid at 90°F. is 143.5 BTU?

   A. 376.5   B. 422.7   C. 467.9   D. 494.8

   5.____

6. The sine of 120° is the same as the sine of

   A. 45°
   B. 60°
   C. 45° but with a negative sign
   D. 60° but with a negative sign

7. In a circular curve of radius R and central angle I, the distance is used to locate the

   A. point of curvature
   B. point of intersection or vertex
   C. center of the curve from the vertex
   D. midpoint of the chord of the circular curve

8. The formula for the area of a triangle is

   A. 1/2ab sin A    B. 1/2bc sin A    C. 1/2ac cos A    D. 1/2ab cosA

9. The logarithm of 7 is approximately 0.845.
   The logarithm of $(0.007)^{1/4}$ is APPROXIMATELY

   A. 9.343-10    B. 9.567-10    C. 9.461-10    D. 9.561-10

10. The center of gravity of a triangle is located at the intersection of the

    A. angle bisectors
    B. medians
    C. perpendicular bisectors of the sides
    D. radians

11. The distance between two stations was measured six times, and the average distance found to be 346.215 ft.
    If one measurement of 351.205 ft. is deleted from the data as being inconsistent with the other measurements, then the average of the remaining five measurements is, in feet,

    A. 345.217    B. 345.221    C. 345.227    D. 345.235

12. A map of an area 380 ft. x 740 ft. is to be plotted on a sheet of drawing paper.
    The SMALLEST sheet of paper required to plot this map to a scale of 1" = 50', leaving a one-inch margin all around, is, in inches,

    A. 8 1/2 x 11    B. 10 x 17    C. 12 x 17    D. 10 x 15

13. On a topographic map, widely spaced contour lines indicate

    A. a gentle slope          B. a steep slope
    C. an overhanging cliff    D. the bank of a stream

14. The scale to which a map is drawn is 1" = 800'.
    IOf the following, the MOST common method by which this scale would be indicated on the map is

    A. 1/800             B. 1" - 9600"
    C. 8.0" = one mile   D. 1/9600

15. The angle formed between one line and the prolongation of the preceding line in a closed traverse is known as _____ angle.   15.____

    A. split  
    B. obtuse  
    C. direction  
    D. deflection

16. When laying out a horizontal circular curve, the deflection angle for a 100 ft. chord is equal to _____ of curvature.   16.____

    A. one-quarter of the degree  
    B. one-half of the degree  
    C. three-quarters of the degree  
    D. the degree

17. For a given intersection angle, tables of the functions of a one degree curve show the tangent distance to be 1062.0 ft.   17.____

    For the same intersection angle and a curvature of 4°, the tangent distance is, in feet, MOST NEARLY

    A. 265.5  B. 437.9  C. 649.3  D. 1153.4

18. Assume that a certain pumping station has three pumps A, B, and C. A can pump 1,000 gallons in 6 minutes, B can pump 1,000 gallons in 3 minutes, and C can pump 1,000 gallons in 2 minutes.   18.____
    The time required for all three pumps working at the same time to pump 1,000 gallons is MOST NEARLY _____. minute(s).

    A. 2  B. 1  C. 14 1/2  D. 1/2

19. Of the following, the equation of a line tangent to the graph of $x^2 + y^2 = 81$ is   19.____

    A. $x = 9$  B. $x + y = 9$  C. $x = 9y$  D. $x = -9y$

20. Of the following, the equation whose roots are -3 and 2 is   20.____

    A. $2x^2 + 3x - 6 = 0$  
    B. $x^2 + x - 6 = 0$  
    C. $x^2 - x + 6 = 0$  
    D. $x^2 + 6 = 0$

21. The sum of 10 1/2, 8 3/4, 51/2, and 2 1/4 is   21.____

    A. 23  B. 25  C. 26  D. 27

22. A water tank measures 50 feet long, 16 feet wide, and 12 feet high. Assume that water weighs 60 pounds per cubic foot and that one gallon of water weighs 8 pounds. The number of gallons the tank can hold when it is half full is   22.____

    A. 21,500  B. 28,375  C. 33,410  D. 36,000

23. Assuming 70 gallons of oil cost $84.00, then 110 gallons of oil at the same rate will cost   23.____

    A. $132.00  B. $168.00  C. $192.00  D. $304.00

24. Three 75-gallon per hour mechanical pressure type oil burners operating together are to burn 150,000 gallons of No. 6 fuel oil.   24.____
    The number of hours they would take to burn this amount of oil is MOST NEARLY

    A. 665  B. 760  C. 870  D. 1210

25. A supplier quotes a list price of $68.00 less discounts of 25 and 20 percent for a replacement part. The actual cost of this item is MOST NEARLY     25.____

   A.  $31        B.  $34        C.  $37        D.  $41

---

## KEY (CORRECT ANSWERS)

1.  D
2.  A
3.  A
4.  B
5.  C

6.  B
7.  C
8.  B
9.  C
10. B

11. A
12. B
13. A
14. D
15. D

16. B
17. A
18. B
19. A
20. B

21. D
22. D
23. A
24. A
25. D

---

# SOLUTIONS TO PROBLEMS

1. 1, 16

2. Mechanical efficiency = 200/250 = 80%

3. Slip = (560 - 500) ÷ 560 = 10.7%

4. Boiler horsepower = (8760)(1.097) ÷ 34.5 ≈ 278

5. BTU = 611.4 - 143.5 = 467.9

6. Sin 120° = sin 60° ≈ .866

7. The distance from the center of a circular curve of radius R from the vertex (central $\angle = I$) is $R(\frac{1}{\cos 1/2 I} - 1)$ = R tan 1/2 tan 1/4 I

8. Area of a triangle = (1/2)(any 2 sides)(sine of the angle between these sides) = 1/2 bc sin A. Other possibilities are 1/2 ab sin C and 1/2 ac sin B.

9. $\text{Log}(.007)^{\frac{1}{4}}$ = 1/4 Log($7 \times 10^{-3}$) = 1/4(Log 7 - 3) ≈ 1/4(.845 - 3) ≈ .539 = 9.461 - 10

10. The medians of a triangle intersect at the center of gravity.

11. (6)(346.215) = 2077.29. Then, (2077.29 - 351.205) 5 = 345.217 ft.

12. 380 ft. is represented by 380/50 = 7.6" and 740 ft. is represented by 740/50 = 14.8". Allowing for a border of 1" on all 4 sides requires a sheet of paper at least 10" x 17"

13. On a topographic map, widely spaced contour lines indicate a gentle slope, while contour lines drawn close together indicate a steep slope.

14. $\frac{1"}{800'} = \frac{1"}{(800)(12)"} = \frac{1}{9600}$

15. A deflection angle is formed between a line and the extension of another line already extant in a closed traverse.

16. One-half of the degree of curvature, by empirical knowledge.

17. The tangent distances are inversely proportional to the curvature angles. Let x = tangent distance. Then, 1062/x = 4/1
    Solving, x = 265.5 ft.

18. Let x = number of minutes when all 3 pumps are working. Then, $1/6x + 1/3x + 1/2x = 1$. Simplifying, $x+2x+3x=6$. Solving, $x = 1$

19. The graph of $x^2 + y^2 = 81$ is a circle with center at (0, 0) and a radius of 9. The line $x = 9$ is vertical and tangent to this circle at (9,0).

20. Given roots -3 and 2, the equation becomes $(x+3)(x-2) = 0$. This is equivalent to $x^2 + x - 6 = 0$

21. 10 1/2 + 8 3/4 + 5 1/2 + 2 1/4 = 25 8/4 = 27

22. Total water weight = (60)(50)(16)(12) = 576,000 pounds.
    Then, 288,000 pounds is the weight when the tank is half full. Finally, 288,000 ÷ 8 = 36,000 gallons

23. Let x = cost. Then, $\dfrac{70}{110} = \dfrac{\$84.00}{x}$. Solving, x = $132.00

24. 150,000 ÷ [(3)(75)] = 666 2/3 hours, closest to 665 hours.

25. Actual cost = ($68.00)(.75)(.80) = $40.80 ≈ $41

# TEST 2

DIRECTIONS: Each question or incomplete statement is followed by several suggested answers or completions. Select the one that BEST answers the question or completes the statement. *PRINT THE LETTER OF THE CORRECT ANSWER IN THE SPACE AT THE RIGHT.*

1. A street has a grade of 1 1/2%.
   The distance the street rises in 1 1/2 miles is MOST NEARLY, in feet,

   A. 79.20  B. 98.75  C. 103.50  D. 118.80

   1._____

2. The signs of the sine, cosine, and tangent of an angle are all positive in Quadrant

   A. I  B. II  C. III  D. IV

   2._____

3. The sum of three interior angles of a four-sided parcel of land add up to 115°.
   The fourth interior angle, in degrees, is

   A. 25  B. 75  C. 245  D. 295

   3._____

4. A circular tank is 12 feet in diameter and 9 feet high. The depth of water in the tank is 1/3 from the top. There are 7 1/2 gallons in a cubic foot.
   The number of gallons of water in the tank is MOST NEARLY

   A. 4,820  B. 5,090  C. 5,320  D. 5,570

   4._____

5. If log of 2 = 0.3010 and log of 3 = 0.4772, then the log of 36 equals

   A. 0.7782  B. 1.0792  C. 1.2554  D. 1.5564

   5._____

6. If there are 43,560 square feet in an acre, the number of acres in a tract 2 miles long by 3.2 miles wide is MOST NEARLY

   A. 3,750  B. 4,100  C. 4,350  D. 4,600

   6._____

7. A foundation for a building consists of 9 concrete footings 8 ft. by 6 ft. by 18 inches deep.
   The total number of cubic yards of concrete in the footings is

   A. 12  B. 24  C. 36  D. 72

   7._____

8. Two applications at 0.4 gallons per square yard of bituminous material on a half mile of road 18 feet wide would require MOST NEARLY _____ gallons.

   A. 425  B. 3,875  C. 4,225  D. 38,000

   8._____

9. Rock excavation is to be paid for at a unit price of $75/cubic yard.
   Of the following, the cost of rock between Sta. 3+35 and Sta. 8+65 for a width of 45 feet and a depth of five feet is MOST NEARLY

   A. $225,000  B. $330,000  C. $660,000  D. $990,000

   9._____

10. Three 40-foot long piles are driven so that their top elevations are 79.6', 81.7', and 80.2' before being cut off at elevation 75.5'.
    If the contract unit price is $13.50 per foot in place, then the payment to the contractor is MOST NEARLY

    A. $1,215.00  B. $1,417.50  C. $1,620.00  D. $1,800.00

    10._____

75

2 (#2)

11. In the sketch shown at the right, the length of X is
    A. 8.0
    B. 9.0
    C. 9.5
    D. 10.0

12. In Circle O, inscribed angle ABC and central angle AOC have the same intercepted arc AC in common.
    Of the following relationships between angle AOC and angle ABC, the one which is TRUE is that

    A. angle ABC equals angle AOC
    B. angle AOC equals one-half angle ABC
    C. angle ABC equals one-half angle AOC
    D. nothing can be said about their relative sizes solely on the basis of the information given

13. The scale of a drawing is 1/8" = 1'0". A rectangle on the drawing actually measures 7 1/8" x 6 1/4".
    This represents the true area in square feet of MOST NEARLY

    A. 72      B. 144      C. 1,375      D. 2,850

14. The length of AB is, in feet, MOST NEARLY
    A. 130
    B. 135
    C. 140
    D. 145

15. An inspector estimated that a paving job would require 20 cubic yards of concrete. The volume of the concrete actually used was 27.5 cubic yards.
    The percentage of error in the inspector's estimate is MOST NEARLY

    A. 40      B. 38      C. 36      D. 34

16. For a 20 foot ladder, the base should extend back from the face of the wall APPROXIMATELY _____ feet.

    A. 3       B. 5        C. 7         D. 10

17. $\frac{\pi}{2}$ radian is equivalent to, in degrees,

    A. 22 1/2  B. 45       C. 90        D. 180

18. The $\sqrt{690}$ is MOST NEARLY

    A. 26.25   B. 26.27    C. 26.29     D. 26.30

19. The line y = 2x + 8 intersects the x axis at

    A.  -4    B.  +4    C.  -2    D.  +8

20. If the radius of the circle shown at the right is 5", the area of the shaded area, in square inches, is MOST NEARLY
    A. 5.1
    B. 7.1
    C. 7.6
    D. 8.1

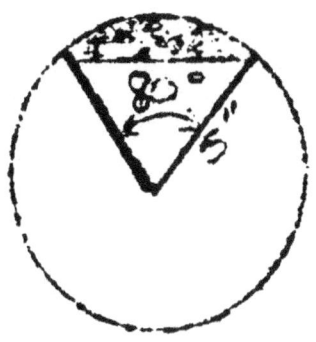

21. A cone has a base whose area is A and its altitude is h. The volume of this cone is

    A.  Ah    B.  1/2Ah    C.  1/3Ah    D.  1/4Ah

22. If $Y = X^{2x}$, the value of Y for X = 3 is

    A.  27    B.  81    C.  243    D.  729

23. The equation $3x^3 - 5x^2 - 15x - 1 = y$ will cross the x axis for values of x between x = _____ and x = _____.

    A.  0; 1    B.  1; 2    C.  2; 3    D.  3; 4

24. The shape of the surface created by a plane cutting the right cone as shown at the right would be a(n)
    A. parabola
    B. hyperbola
    C. ellipse
    D. circle

25. The area of the shaded part of the circle shown at the right is MOST NEARLY
    A. 6.1
    B. 7.1
    C. 8.1
    D. 9.1

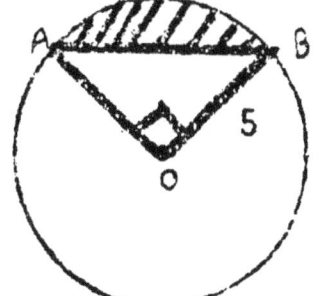

## KEY (CORRECT ANSWERS)

1. D
2. A
3. C
4. B
5. D

6. B
7. B
8. C
9. B
10. B

11. D
12. C
13. D
14. B
15. B

16. B
17. C
18. B
19. A
20. A

21. C
22. D
23. D
24. C
25. B

# SOLUTIONS TO PROBLEMS

1. Let x = required distance. Then, x/7920 = .015 . So, x = 118.80 ft.
   Note: 1 1/2 mi. = (1 1/2)(5280) = 7920 ft.

2. In Quadrant I, sine, cosine, tangent of any angle is positive.

3. The 4th angle = $360° - 115° = 245°$

4. Volume of water = $(2/3)(\pi)(6^2)(9) = 216\pi$ cu.ft. Then, $(7.5)(216\pi) \approx 5091$ gallons, closest to 5090 gallons.

5. Log 36 = $\text{Log}(2^2 \cdot 3^2)$ = 2Log 2 + 2Log 3 = 2(.3010) + 2(.4772) = 1.5564

6. (2)(3.2) = 6.4 sq.miles = (6.4)(5280)(5280) = 178,421,760 sq.ft.
   Then, 178,421,760 ÷ 43,560 = 4096, closest to 4100 acres.

7. (9)(8')(6')(1 1/2') = 648 cu.ft. = 648/27 = 24 cu.yds.

8. (1/2 mi.)(18 ft.) = (880 yds.)(6 yds.) = 5280 sq.yds. Two applications requires (5280)(.4)(2) = 4224, closest to 4225 gallons.

9. 865 - 335 = 530. Then, (530)(45)(5) = 119,250 cu.ft. = 4416 2/3 cu.yds. Finally, ($75)(4416 2/3) = $331,250, which is closest to $330,000.

10. (75.5' - 40')(3) = 106.5'. Then, (106.5)($13.50) = $1437.75, which is closest to $1417.50

11. $\dfrac{EC}{EB} = \dfrac{GC}{AB}$, so $\dfrac{12}{18} = \dfrac{GC}{12}$ = 8. Now, $(BC)^2 + (GC)^2 = (GB)^2$, so $36 + 64 = (GB)^2$. Solving, GB = 10

12. ∠ADC = intercept arc in degrees and ∠ABC = 1/2 times the intercepted arc. Thus, <ABC = (1/2)(∠ADC)

13. 7 1/8" x 6 1/4" is actually (57)(50) = 2850 sq.ft.

14. Draw $\overline{AC} // \overline{ED}$, so that △ACB has a right angle at C.
    BC = 60' - 10' = 50', AC = ED = 125'. Now, $125^2 + 50^2 = (AB)^2$. Solving, AB = $\sqrt{18,125} \approx 135$ ft.

15. (27.5 - 20) ÷ 20 = 37 1/2% ≈ 38%

16. For safety, the angle of elevation between the ladder and the ground should be 75°. Let x = required distance. Then,
    cos 75° = x/20 Solving, x ≈ 5 ft.

17. $\frac{\pi}{2}$ radians $= (\frac{\pi}{2})\frac{180}{\pi} = 90°$

18. $\sqrt{690} \approx 26.27$

19. Let y = 0 in the equation y = 2x + 8. Then, 0 = 2x + 8, so x = -4

20. Area of entire circle = $(\pi)(5^2) = 25\pi$. If the central angle is 80°, the area of the sector bounded by A, O, B = $(25\pi)(80/360) = 5.\overline{5}\pi$. Area of $\triangle AOB = [(1/2)(AO)(OB)(\sin 80°)] = (1/2)(5)(5)(\sin 80°) \approx 12.31$. Finally, the shaded area = $5.5\pi - 12.31 \approx 5.14 \approx 5.1$ sq.in.

21. V = 1/3 Ah for the volume of a cone with base area of A and a height of h.

22. $Y = 3^{2 \cdot 3} = 3^6 = 729$

23. Given $y = 3x^3 - 5x^2 - 15x - 1$, the values of y for x = 0, 1, 2, 3, and 4 are: -1, -18, -12, -10, and 51, respectively. Since the graph must cross the x-axis whenever the y value changes sign, this will take place between x = 3 and x = 4. (Incidentally, the graph also crosses the x-axis at approximately x = -.1 and x = -1.5)

24. Whenever a plane cuts a right circular cone at an acute angle, the surface created is an ellipse.

25. Area of sector AOB = $(1/4)(\pi)(25) = 6.25\pi$. Area of $\triangle ADB = (1/2)(5)(5) = 12.5$. Finally, shaded area = $6.25\pi - 12.5 \approx 7.1$

# TEST 3

DIRECTIONS: Each question or incomplete statement is followed by several suggested answers or completions. Select the one that BEST answers the question or completes the statement. *PRINT THE LETTER OF THE CORRECT ANSWER IN THE SPACE AT THE RIGHT.*

1. The equation $\frac{x^2}{a^2} - \frac{y^2}{b^2} = 1$ is the formula for a(n)

   A. cantenary   B. ellipse   C. hyperbola   D. cycloid

2. A pile plan shows fifteen concrete-filled 18" inside diameter steel piles each 35 feet long. If the cost of concrete in place is $120 a cubic yard, then the total cost of the concrete in the piles is MOST NEARLY

   A. $3,750   B. $4,140   C. $4,350   D. $4,500

3. The coverage of a gallon of paint is 400 square feet. The MINIMUM number of gallons required to paint four walls of four rooms each 18 feet by 16 feet by 8 feet high is

   A. 4   B. 5   C. 6   D. 7

4. If there are 22 bricks in a square foot of a 12 inch thick wall, then the number of bricks in a 6 foot wall around a parcel of land 32 feet by 110 feet is MOST NEARLY

   A. 37,000   B. 37,250   C. 37,500   D. 37,750

5. The number of significant figures in 0.0000556 is

   A. 2   B. 3   C. 4   D. 5

6. 

   In the sketch shown above, the number of feet in the perimeter is MOST NEARLY

   A. 100   B. 105   C. 115   D. 122

7. If the central angle of a circle is 1/3 of a radian, then the number of degrees in the central angle is MOST NEARLY

   A. 6   B. 9.5   C. 12   D. 19

8. The $\sqrt{465}$ is MOST NEARLY

   A. 20.56   B. 21.13   C. 21.34   D. 21.56

9. 90° is MOST NEARLY equal to _____ radians.

   A. 0.5   B. 1.5   C. 2.5   D. 3.5

10. When .68 feet is converted to inches, the result is MOST NEARLY

   A. 7 7/8"   B. 8"   C. 8 1/8"   D. 8 1/4"

11. A 100' guy wire, stretched tight from the top of a vertical pole, makes a 60° angle with the level ground.
    The height of this pole, in feet, is MOST NEARLY (sin 60° = .867; cos 60° = .500)

   A. 50   B. 87   C. 100   D. 200

12. The area of a 120° sector of a circle whose radius is 3" is MOST NEARLY _____ square inches.

   A. 7.9   B. 9.42   C. 11.3   D. 12.5

13. The product $\dfrac{6xy}{(x^2-4)} \cdot \dfrac{5x-10)}{3xy}$ is equal to

   A. $\dfrac{2xy}{x^2-10}$   B. $\dfrac{30x^2}{x^2 y}$   C. $\dfrac{10}{x+2}$   D. $\dfrac{18x^3 y}{x+10}$

14. The $\sin^2 x$ is equal to

   A. $1 - 2\cos^2 x$   B. $1 + 2\cos^2 x$
   C. $1 + \cos^2 x$   D. $1 - \cos^2 x$

15. The volume of a cylinder with a radius r and height h is

   A. $\pi r^2 h$   B. $2\pi r h$   C. $2\pi r^2 h$   D. $4\pi r^2 h$

16. The expression reduces to

   A. $\sqrt{7}$   B. $3\sqrt{7}$   C. $\sqrt{21}$   D. $-\sqrt{35}$

17. If sin 2x = 1, then x is

   A. 30°   B. 45°   C. 60°   D. 75°

18. The expression $\dfrac{x^2 y^2}{y} \cdot \dfrac{x^2}{x^4} + y^0$ reduces to

   A. $\dfrac{xy}{x^4}$   B. $\dfrac{y^2}{y-x^4}$   C. $\dfrac{y-1}{x^2}+1$   D. $\dfrac{y-1}{x^2+y}$

19. If the coordinates of E and F in the X-Y plane are (1,-1) and (4,3), respectively, then the length of line E - F is

   A. 4   B. 5   C. 6   D. 7

20. If there are 43,560 square feet in an acre and 640 acres in a square mile, then the number of acres in a tract of land 2640 feet by 7920 feet is MOST NEARLY

    A. 640  B. 480  C. 360  D. 10

21. Point B is 3 miles north and 4 miles east of point A. A person traveling in a straight line from A to B and back again to A would travel a distance EQUAL to _____ miles.

    A. 14  B. 12  C. 10  D. 5

22. The flow from a wide open fire hydrant is 300 gallons per minute. When the hydrant is equipped with a spray nozzle, the flow is reduced to 20 gallons per minute. Over a period of 8 hours, the quantity of water saved by installing a spray nozzle is MOST NEARLY _____ gallons.

    A. 146,200  B. 134,400  C. 56,500  D. 2,400

23. A rectangular building is 100 feet long and 40 feet wide. Waterproofing is to be applied to the exterior of the 10-foot high basement walls at the rate of 2.5 gallons per 100 square feet of wall.
    The number of gallons of waterproofing requires is MOST NEARLY

    A. 70  B. 60  C. 28  D. 10

24. An angle is measured 4 times, and the total of the four readings is 186° 41'22". The angle is MOST NEARLY

    A. 47° 10'12.0"  B. 46° 40'20.5"
    C. 46° 32'17.6"  D. 45° 30'15.4"

25. A square tract of land contains 57,600 square feet. The length of a fence needed to enclose the entire property is MOST NEARLY _____ feet.

    A. 960  B. 752  C. 480  D. 300

## 4 (#3)
## KEY (CORRECT ANSWERS)

1. C
2. B
3. C
4. C
5. B

6. D
7. D
8. D
9. B
10. C

11. B
12. B
13. C
14. D
15. A

16. A
17. B
18. C
19. B
20. B

21. C
22. B
23. A
24. B
25. A

———

# SOLUTIONS TO PROBLEMS

1. $\dfrac{x^2}{a^2} - \dfrac{y^2}{b^2} = 1$ represents a hyperbola with vertices at $(\pm a, 0)$ and foci at $(\pm c, 0)$, where $c^2 = a^2 + b^2$

2. Total volume (in cu.ft.) of all 15 piles = $(15)(\pi)(.75)(.75)(35) = 295.3125\pi \approx 927.75$.
   Converting to cu.yds., $927.75 \div 27 \approx 34.36$.
   Finally, $(34.36)(\$120) \approx \$4123$, closest to $4140

3. 544 sq.ft. x 4 rooms = 2176 ÷ 400 = 5.4 gallons = 6 gallons

4. Total wall area = $(2)(6)(32) + (2)(6)(110) = 1704$ sq.ft. Then, $(1704)(22) = 37{,}488$ bricks, closest to 37,500 bricks.

5. .0000556 has 3 significant (non-zero) figures.

6. AD = $(15)/(\sin 60°) \approx 17$ ft., BC = $(15)/(\sin 30°) = 30$ ft., DE = $15/(\tan 60°) \approx 9$ ft., and FC = $15/(\tan 30°)$ 26 ft.
   Thus, DC $\approx 9 + 20 + 26 = 55$ ft. Perimeter of ABCD = $20 + 30 + 55 + 17 = 122$ ft.

7. 1/3 radian = $(1/3)\dfrac{180}{\pi} = \dfrac{60}{\pi}$ ~ 19 degrees

8. $\sqrt{465} \approx 21.56$

9. $90° = 1/2\,\pi$ radians $\approx 1.57$ radians, closest to 1.5 radians

10. .68 ft. = (.68)(12) = 8.16 in., closest to 8 1/8 in.

11. Let x = height of pole. Then, $\sin 60° = x/100$ This becomes $.867 = x/100$. Solving, $x \approx 87$ ft.

12. Area of 120° sector = (1/3)(area of circle) = $(1/3)(\pi)(3^2)$ 9.42 sq.in.

13. $\dfrac{6xy}{(x-2)(x+2)} \cdot \dfrac{5(x-2)}{3xy} = \dfrac{10}{(x-2)}$

14. $\sin^2 x = 1 - \cos^2 x$ always

15. $V = \pi r^2 h$ is the volume of a cylinder with radius = r and height = h

16. $\sqrt{28} - \sqrt{7} = \sqrt{4 \cdot 7} - \sqrt{7} = 2\sqrt{7} - \sqrt{7} = \sqrt{7}$

17. If $\sin 2x = 1$, then $2x = 90°$, so $x = 45°$

18. $\dfrac{x^{-2}y^2}{y} - \dfrac{x^2}{x^4} + y^0 = \dfrac{y}{x^2} - \dfrac{1}{x^2} + 1 = \dfrac{y-1}{x^2} + 1$

19. $EF = \sqrt{(1-4)^2 + (-1-3)^2} = \sqrt{9+16} = 5$

20. $(2640')(7920') = 20{,}908{,}800$ sq.ft. Then, $20{,}908{,}800 \div 43{,}560 = 480$ acres.

21. $A \to B = \sqrt{3^2 + 4^2} = 5$, so the distance back and forth = 10 miles

22. $(300-20)(60)(8) = 134{,}400$ gallons

23. Total surface area = $(2)(100')(10') + (2)(40')(10') = 2800$ sq.ft.
    Let x = number of gallons. Then, $2.5/100 = x/2800$ Solving, $x = 70$

24. $186°41'22'' \div 4 = 672{,}082'' \div 4 = 168{,}020.5'' \approx 46.672° \approx 46°40'19''$, closest to $46°40'20.5''$

25. Each side = $\sqrt{57{,}600 \text{ sq.ft.}} = 240$ ft.
    Perimeter = $(4)(240) = 960$ ft.

# THEORY OF HEAT

## CONTENTS

|  |  | Page |
|---|---|---|
| A. | INTRODUCTION | 1 |
| B. | MEASUREMENT OF HEAT | 1 |
| C. | KINDS OF HEAT | 2 |
| D. | PRESSURE | 4 |
| E. | VAPORIZATION | 6 |
| F. | PHYSICAL CONDITIONS OF VAPORS AND LIQUIDS | 7 |
| G. | EXPANSION AND CONTRACTION OF SUBSTANCE | 7 |
| H. | HEAT TRANSFER | 8 |
| I. | INSULATION | 9 |

# THEORY OF HEAT

## A. INTRODUCTION

A1. General.—As mentioned earlier, heat is a very relative term. Usually one thinks of it as a means of warming the body, or some object, to a desired temperature. Strange as it may seem, heat is ever present, even in a block of ice. In this chapter, heat is explained in terms of how it is used and transferred from substance to substance. Heat transfer is what all refrigeration systems are designed to accomplish. To understand the basic principles of refrigeration, it is most important that the student have a definite understanding of the relationship of heat, temperatures, and pressures.

A2. Matter Defined.—Matter is anything that has weight and occupies space. All substances are forms of matter in one of three stages: solid, liquid, or gaseous. An example of a substance in its three stages is water.

In its natural state water is a liquid. It has weight, volume, and takes the shape of the container which holds it. If it is heated in a closed container to its boiling point and more heat is added, it changes to steam or vapor which is its gaseous state. It has weight and occupies the volume or space of the container. When water is frozen, it becomes ice or is in its solid state. In this state, it has weight and volume, and it takes a definite shape.

Theoretically, all substances can be converted from one to another of the three states by the addition or withdrawal of heat. However, chemical compounds differ in the ease or difficulty with which they may be changed from one to another of the three physical states. Some, like water, can very readily be converted into each of the three states; others, like paper, oxidize, or burn, at high temperatures and cannot be converted into all three. Before paper burns, it changes to a gas, but never to a liquid. The science of refrigeration depends upon changes in physical state through heating or cooling.

A3. Definition of Heat.—Heat is a form of energy. It cannot be seen or shaped, nor can it be created or destroyed. It can only be transferred from substance to substance.

All substances are made up of tiny molecules. These molecules are in constant motion and moving against each other. As the temperature of these molecules increases, so does their activity, and as heat is taken away their activity and temperature decrease. If all heat is extracted from a substance (absolute zero temperature), the molecular motion will become dormant.

## B. MEASUREMENT OF HEAT

B1. Intensity and Quantity.—From experience we know that heat and temperature are related. If heat is added to a substance the temperature of the substance will rise, and if heat is taken away the temperature will decrease. There is a difference, however, in quantity and intensity. Heat is measured (1) by its intensity, and (2) by the quantity of it possessed by a substance. This is readily understood by comparing a spoonful of hot water with a pailful of warm water. The hot water in the spoon has a greater intensity of heat, but the warm water in the pail possesses a larger quantity of heat, though at a lower intensity.

B2. Thermometer.—Intensity of heat is measured by the ordinary thermometer with which everyone is familiar. The two methods of dividing and numbering the thermometer scales in common use are the Fahrenheit and the Centigrade. Another scale not so common but used by scientists is the Kelvin.

B3. Fahrenheit Scale.—The temperature scale most commonly used in refrigeration is the Fahrenheit scale represented by the designator °F. This scale is fixed to divide the

## THEORY OF HEAT

difference between melting ice and boiling water into 180 equal degrees. The melting ice is represented by a mark of 32° F, and boiling water at 212° F. Degrees above and below these are also equal divisions shown on the scale. When reaching the temperature where all molecular action in all substances ceases, a thermometer reading of -459.69° F would be indicated. This is called absolute zero. Scientists have been able, under controlled conditions, to measure temperatures within a few thousandths of absolute zero.

**B4. Centigrade Scale.**—The centigrade thermometer is scaled in degrees and indicated by °C. On this scale, ice melts at 0° C and water boils at 100° C. The 100 degrees between melting point and boiling point are equally divided on the scale. The absolute zero temperature on the centigrade scale is -273.16° C.

The centigrade scaled thermometer is used in most countries except the United States and Britain. It is used universally in scientific work.

**B5. Absolute or Kelvin Scale.**—The Kelvin scale is graduated in degrees starting at zero. On this scale, 0° K is equal to -273° C or -460° F, or absolute zero. The boiling point of water, 373° K, and the melting point of ice, 273° K, are equal to readings on the Fahrenheit and centigrade scales as shown in figure 1.

**B6. British Thermal Unit.**—The quantity of heat possessed by a substance is measured in terms of the British thermal unit, abbreviated Btu. A Btu is the quantity of heat required to raise the temperature of one pound of pure water one degree Fahrenheit at or near 39.10° F. This is the temperature at which water is at maximum density. For example, to raise the temperature of five pounds of water from 39° to 49° F, or from 160° to 170° F, requires $5 \times 10 = 50$ Btu. For all practical purposes, the Btu is considered constant between 32° and 212° F, though it does vary a slight amount.

## C. KINDS OF HEAT

**C1. General.**—To have an understanding of the terminology used in refrigeration and air conditioning, it is essential that the meaning of the terms discussed in this section be known. Some terms seem closely related, but the meaning and way they are applied is very important. The terms considered here apply to heat.

Figure 1.—Comparison of Fahrenheit, centigrade, and Kelvin temperature scales.

**C2. Specific Heat.**—Specific heat is the number of Btu that must be added to a unit weight of substance to raise its temperature 1 degree Fahrenheit. Since most substances held to a constant weight vary in volume, varying numbers of Btu are required to change the temperature 1 degree Fahrenheit per unit.

Technically, the specific heat of a substance is the ratio of the amount of heat required to change the temperature of a unit weight of that substance 1 degree to the amount of heat required to change the temperature of the same weight of water one degree. Since the specific heat of water is, by definition, equal to 1, the specific heat of other substances are expressed as decimals. Examples of the specific heat of some substances follow:

| Material | Specific Heat (Btu/Lb) |
|---|---|
| Wood | .327 |
| Ice | .504 |
| Iron | .129 |
| Copper | .095 |
| Glass | .187 |

| | |
|---|---|
| Mercury | .033 |
| Alcohol | .615 |
| Liquid Ammonia at 40° F. | 1.100 |

**C3. Thermal Capacity.**—Thermal capacity is closely related to specific heat. The specific heat of a substance is the number of Btu necessary to raise the temperature of one pound of the substance one degree Fahrenheit. The thermal capacity of a substance is the amount of heat required to raise the temperature of its whole mass one degree. Hence, thermal capacity equals the specific heat of a substance multiplied by its mass. Thermal capacity may be said to express the total capacity of a given quantity of a substance for absorbing and storing heat. Thermal capacity is stated, not as a ratio, but as a certain number of Btu.

**C4. Sensible Heat.**—Heat that is added to, or subtracted from, a substance that changes its temperature but not its physical state is called sensible heat. It is the heat that can be indicated on a thermometer. This is the heat which human senses also can react to, at least within certain ranges. For example, if a person puts his finger into a cup of water, his senses readily tell him whether it is cold, cool, tepid, hot, or very hot. Human senses are not sufficiently discriminating to give precise information about the extreme temperatures of ice and steam or other substances having temperatures beyond the range of human sensory mechanisms. Ice merely seems cold and steam seems hot whatever their temperatures. Sensible heat is applied to a solid (as ice), a liquid (as water), or a vapor/gas (as steam) as indicated on a thermometer. The term sensible heat does not apply to the process of conversion from one physical state to another.

**C5. Latent Heat.**—Heat absorbed, or given up, during the conversion of a substance from one physical state to another has another name. This is called latent heat. The term, latent heat, has two forms; latent heat of fusion and latent heat of vaporization.

Latent is taken from the Greek language meaning hidden. When latent heat is added to or subtracted from a substance, and the physical change takes place, there is no change in the sensible heat or temperature of the substance.

**C6. Latent Heat of Fusion.**—If heat is applied to a piece of ice at a temperature of 0° F, the temperature of the ice would gradually rise. This change in temperature, which can be indicated by placing a thermometer on the ice, is called sensible heat as stated previously. No change in state takes place, only a change in the temperature of the ice.

As more sensible heat is added, the temperature of the ice finally reaches 32° F. Now, as more heat is absorbed by the ice, the ice melts or changes state, but the temperature of the liquid is also 32° F. The heat added during the process of melting the ice at 32° to water at 32° F (at sea level barometric pressure) is the hidden or latent heat of fusion.

This process also works in the reverse order. When water is chilled to 32° F and more heat is taken away to form it into ice at 32° F, this heat is also latent heat of fusion.

Here is where one of the most important laws in physics is involved in refrigeration; heat can never be destroyed. It can only be transferred from one substance to another. So, the same amount of heat required to melt the ice into water must be removed from the water to convert it back to ice.

The latent heat of fusion for pure water at 32° F and at sea-level barometric pressure is 143.33 Btu per pound.

**C7. Latent Heat of Vaporization.**—As the last of the ice melts, the temperature of the water begins to rise. The temperature causing the rise is sensible heat. When the temperature of water reaches 212° F, the temperature stops rising and another change takes place. More heat is added and the water boils or changes to steam, but there is no change in temperature. This too is hidden heat. As the last of the water vaporizes and more heat is added, the temperature will again rise and again we are dealing with sensible heat.

The heat added to, or taken away, in the process of changing water to steam vapor, or from vapor/steam back to water, is called latent heat of vaporization. All substances that change from liquid to a vapor or gas go through this stage.

The value set for one pound of water at 212° F to be converted into steam, or steam converted to water, is 970.4 Btu. Other changes of state with variation of temperature, and the number of Btu required by such changes for a pound of water, are shown in figure 2.

# THEORY OF HEAT

Figure 2.—Relationship between sensible heat and latent heat for water at atmospheric pressure.

C8. Total Heat.—The term total heat is used with two different meanings and care must be used in reading textbooks in order that the meaning intended is properly understood. These two usages are as follows:

Strictly speaking, the total heat of a substance is the total heat energy calculated from absolute zero in Btu. It is specific heat x mass x absolute temperature. Since there is no instrument, however, for measuring heat directly on the absolute scale, and since it would also require high numbers, other starting points are arbitrarily chosen. For the liquid water, the arbitrary starting point is 32° F.

In refrigeration and air conditioning, the total heat of a substance or of the air in a room is all the heat present, that is:

Total Heat = Sensible Heat + Latent Heat

In discussions, the term heat content is sometimes used. This term has the same meaning as total heat.

## D. PRESSURE

D1. Atmospheric Pressure.—At the beginning of this chapter, we defined matter as anything which occupies space and has weight. As air is matter, it too has weight. The weight of this air is called atmospheric pressure. The valued scale for a column of air 1 inch square in cross-sectional area at the base and reaching from sea level to the upper limit of the earth's atmosphere at 32° F and at sea level is 14.696 pounds. This will vary due to condition changes in the air above the earth. For all practical purposes, the value is considered to be 14.7 pounds per square inch (psi) at sea level.

D2. **Mercury Barometer.**—To measure atmospheric pressure, scientists have developed a simple instrument called a mercury barometer. It is constructed with a glass tube that is a little over thirty inches long and sealed at one end. The tube is then completely filled with mercury. By placing a finger over the open end and inverting into an open dish of mercury, the mercury column in the tube will fall, leaving a vacuum in the space above the mercury. The air pressure exerted on the surface of the mercury in the dish will maintain a column of mercury in the tube equal to the pressure at the surface. At sea level pressure of 14.7 psi, the height of the column of mercury in the tube will be 29.921 inches. As atmospheric pressure is increased or decreased, the height of the mercury column will vary in relation to the pressure.

D3. **Aneroid Barometer.**—Another device used to measure atmospheric pressure is the aneroid barometer. This type is more compact and easier to handle than the mercury barometer, but not as accurate.

The aneroid barometer consists of an airtight metal box, with a partial vacuum inside, and a flexible side that can move slightly under varying pressures. The motion of the flexible side is transmitted through gears and levers to a pointer that is calibrated to a scale on the dial. This scale is graduated in inches and corresponds to the inches of mercury in the mercury barometer.

A good aneroid barometer will show a slight increase in pressure when lowered from a table to the floor.

D4. **Conversion of Barometer Readings.**—Since the aneroid and mercury barometers indicate the atmospheric pressure in inches, a conversion factor must be used to convert this pressure to pounds per square inch. At an air temperature of 32° F and at mean sea level, the mercury column stands at 29.921 inches and corresponds to a pressure of 14.696 psi. By dividing 14.696 by 29.921, the result will give the conversion factor of 0.491. To convert the reading on the barometer, multiply the reading by the conversion factor.

D5. **Variation of Pressure and Boiling Point with Altitude.**—The pressures and boiling points of substances will vary with altitudes. If an uncovered container filled with fresh water at mean sea level is heated until the water boils, a thermometer inserted in the water shows that its temperature is 212° F, and a barometer shows that the atmospheric pressure is approximately 14.7 psi. However, if the pot of boiling water is on a hilltop 1000 feet above sea level, the thermometer shows that the water boils at 210° F when the barometer reads approximately 14.14 psi. Similar variations in boiling point and barometric pressure are observed at different altitudes, as indicated in the following table:

| Feet above sea level | Pressure (psi) | Boiling point of Water (°F) |
| --- | --- | --- |
| Sea level | 14.70 | 212 |
| 2000 | 13.57 | 208 |
| 4000 | 12.49 | 204 |
| 6000 | 11.54 | 200 |
| 8000 | 10.62 | 196 |

D6. **Pressure-Temperature Relationship for Change of State.**—It is not variations of pressure and temperatures at different altitudes to which special attention is directed, but the relationship between the temperature of vaporization and the corresponding pressure. It is not necessary, however, to go to different heights to obtain different pressures; different pressures may be obtained by mechanical means at any location.

For example, a boiling liquid and its vapor may be contained in an airtight metal cylinder with a piston. By moving the piston in or out, the pressure within may be increased or decreased. If the piston is pushed in, thus increasing the pressure inside, a thermometer shows that the change of state from liquid to vapor requires a temperature higher than 212° F. If the piston is pulled out, thus decreasing the pressure within, the thermometer shows that the change of state from liquid to vapor takes

## THEORY OF HEAT

place at a temperature lower than 212° F. Many types of such mechanical arrangements are in common use.

This relationship of vaporization temperature and pressure, which varies for different substances, follows an exact law, and may be tabulated accurately for each substance.

**D7. Pressure Gage.**—Pressures within an airtight system of pipes, tanks, and cylinders are usually measured by a Bourdon-tube pressure gage. In this gage there is a small tube, flattened (not round) in cross-section, and curved to about three-quarters of a circle. One end of this curved tube is firmly fixed to the mounting, or case; the other end is free and slightly movable. A delicate lever system which turns a pointer on a circular scale is attached to the free end. The fixed end of this tube is joined by connections to the vapor system, and made part of that system. Increases in vapor pressure tend to straighten the curved tube, thus rotating the pointer. The scale is marked to indicate the pressure values in units of pounds per square inch.

The scale on the Bourdon-tube pressure gage is marked with zero to correspond to standard atmospheric pressure. Consequently, zero gage pressure equals 14.7 pounds per square inch. When the pressure of the vapor inside the curved tube is 14.7 psi, it is equal to the atmospheric pressure outside the tube, and there is no tendency for the curved tube to straighten. Hence, this pressure is taken as the zero point on the gage.

**D8. Gage Pressure.**—The pressure indicated by a Bourdon-tube pressure gage is in reality the difference between the vapor pressure inside and the air pressure outside the curved tube. Readings from such a gage are always designated gage pressure.

Gage pressure is expressed in pounds per square inch. For convenience, this term is indicated by its abbreviated form psi. Often, where the meaning is unmistakable, the word pounds alone is used; for example, 20 pounds' pressure means 20 pounds per square inch pressure.

**D9. Absolute Pressure.**—The term absolute pressure is used to designate the true total pressure inside the enclosed vapor system. Suppose the pressure gage stands at 6 pounds. Then, since zero gage pressure means 14.7 pounds inside (to balance 14.7 pounds air pressure outside the tube), the total, or absolute pressure of the vapor is 14.7 pounds plus 6 pounds, or 20.7 pounds. If an accurate knowledge of the pressure is required, the atmospheric pressure, converted from a barometer reading, is used instead of the 14.7-pound standard.

**D10. Vacuum or Negative Gage Pressure.**—As stated, the standard atmospheric pressure of 14.7 psi is taken as the zero point on the gage. A gage dealing only with increases in pressure has a single scale marked from 0 to 300 pounds, or some other upper limit, and is read in psi gage pressure.

But, pressures may decrease below atmospheric pressure as well as increase. Pressures below 14.7 psi are known as partial vacuums. This term is merely for convenience in referring to pressures below ordinary atmospheric pressure, since such a pressure is far from approaching a vacuum.

A gage that registers pressures lower than standard atmospheric pressure is called a vacuum gage. Such gages are graduated to read in inches of vacuum. Approximately 30 inches of vacuum equal zero pounds absolute pressure.

**D11. Compound Gage.**—A compound gage is sometimes called a compound pressure and vacuum gage. It has an extended range covering pressures both below and above atmospheric pressure. The scale is graduated to the left and right of zero (atmospheric pressure). Above atmospheric pressure readings are in psi, and below atmospheric pressures are readings of inches of vacuum.

Gages used on the suction side of most refrigeration units are of the compound type.

## E. VAPORIZATION

**E1. Kinds of Vaporization.**—Ebullition, evaporation, and sublimation are the three kinds of vaporization, or methods of converting from one physical state to another.

**E2. Ebullition.**—Ebullition is the technical term for ordinary boiling. It is a rapid and visible process. By looking into an uncovered container of boiling water, one can see that ebullition, or boiling, is taking place. Starting from the bottom and sides, large and small bubbles rise to the surface and escape from the liquid.

E3. **Evaporation.**—Evaporation is a slow and invisible process which takes place only from the surface of a liquid. Under ordinary conditions, evaporation cannot be seen. Any liquid in an uncovered container will gradually evaporate, its level slowly falling until all liquid is gone. Water continually evaporates from the surface of all open bodies such as rivers, lakes, ponds, and oceans. Wet clothing, hung on a line to dry, does so, by this process.

Since evaporation is a form of vaporization, it results in the removal of latent heat. Therefore, it is a cooling process, though a slow one. When a person goes in swimming on a cool day with a wind blowing, it is the evaporation process that makes him feel uncomfortable, rather than the temperature itself. The human body gets rid of excess heat and moisture naturally and continually by evaporation.

Some liquids evaporate much faster than others. For example, alcohol will evaporate much faster than water.

E4. **Sublimation.**—The third method of converting from one physical state to another is called sublimation. It consists of converting from a solid directly to the vapor state without passing through the intermediate or liquid state. Ice and snow, even when much below the freezing point, slowly disappear without melting. Washed clothes, hung out-of-doors in temperatures below 32° F, first freeze stiff, and then dry soft. Both these phenomena are caused by sublimation.

Sublimation has little application to refrigeration engineering. It has, however, considerable use in the small scale cooling of bottled goods, ice cream, and other food stuffs by the use of solid carbon dioxide, or dry ice, which sublimes to a vapor under atmospheric pressure.

E5. **Vapor and Gas.**—The terms vapor and gas both refer to matter in the physical state that is neither solid or liquid. There is, however, a definite distinction between the two.

Vapor condenses very readily to a liquid state under small changes of temperature or pressure, or both, and constantly does so under ordinary conditions of nature. It may be said to be very close to the liquid state, although it is a vapor.

Gas, on the other hand, exists under ordinary conditions in a gaseous state. To change it to a liquid state, special laboratory apparatus capable of producing extreme changes of pressure is required. A gas may be said to be far removed from the liquid state and cannot change under ordinary natural conditions.

In refrigeration, the word gas is frequently used instead of the more correct term vapor.

F. **PHYSICAL CONDITIONS OF VAPORS AND LIQUIDS**

F1. **State and Condition.**—The term state is used to refer to the three forms of matter: solid, liquid, and gas or vapor. However, a substance in any one of the three states may be found in different conditions. Hence, the term condition is also used. A vapor ordinarily exists in either of two conditions, as a saturated vapor or as superheated vapor.

F2. **Saturated Vapor.**—The saturated vapor is a vapor at the temperature corresponding to its boiling point at a given pressure. Saturated vapors are classed as either wet or dry. If they contain liquid particles of their substance, they are termed wet. If no particles are present, they are termed dry.

Saturated vapors are usually in the wet state due to the boiling action of the substance. The bubbles, as they break away from the surface as a vapor, will carry tiny droplets of the liquid suspended in the vapor.

F3. **Superheated Vapor.**—If a vapor is not in contact with a boiling liquid, either because the liquid has been converted into vapor or because the vapor has been separated from the boiling liquid, further application of heat produces a rise in temperature of the vapor under the same given pressure. Such a vapor is called superheated vapor.

F4. **Saturation Temperature.**—If a liquid is heated, it finally boils at a temperature that is the result of the pressure present. Such a temperature is called the saturation temperature corresponding to the given pressure. This term is frequently used in air conditioning and means the boiling point, or the condensation point, at the given pressure.

A liquid that is at the saturation temperature corresponding to a given pressure, and is under that pressure, is called a saturated liquid.

G. **EXPANSION AND CONTRACTION OF SUBSTANCE**

G.1. **General.**—In general, all substances, whether solid, liquid, or gas, decrease in volume

## THEORY OF HEAT

when cooled and increase in volume when heated. In gases and vapors, the amount of change is large; in liquids and solids it is small. In all cases, great forces are produced and it is necessary in all engineering construction to allow for the operation of these forces. Different substances vary in the amount of change in volume they undergo for the same differences in temperature.

G2. **Expansion and Contraction of Water.**—Water contracts as it is cooled until the temperature 39.2°F is reached. At this point the change in volume reverses and if the water is cooled further, the volume increases. When water freezes into ice, an enormous force is brought into play. This force is sufficient to split large rocks, burst iron pipes and even steel tanks, unless provisions are allowed for the expansion.

G3. **Expansion and Contraction at the Change of State.**—At their melting point, substances follow no general rule regarding expansion and contraction. Some metals like iron, bismuth, and antimony, contract on melting and expand on solidifying; but most others like gold, silver, and copper, expand on melting and contract on solidifying. All liquids, however, expand greatly when changing into a vapor unless constrained mechanically, as in a closed container. An example of this expansion is the large clouds of steam continually rising from a container of boiling water.

G4. **Specific Volume.**—The specific volume of a substance is a number that indicates the number of cubic feet occupied by one pound of the substance at a given temperature and pressure. Specific volume varies greatly for different substances and for the same substances at different temperatures and pressures.

The specific volume for boiling water at atmospheric pressure is 0.0167 cubic feet per pound, and of steam at the same pressure it is 26.79 cubic feet per pound. Thus, water in changing its state from liquid to vapor at ordinary atmospheric pressure increases in volume 1604 times.

## H. HEAT TRANSFER

H1. **How Heat is Transferred.**—As explained earlier in this chapter, heat can neither be created nor destroyed, but only transferred from one substance to another. This transfer is accomplished through one of three ways: radiation, convection, and conduction.

H2. **Radiation.**—In radiation, heat is transmitted through empty space (a vacuum), as from the sun to the earth's atmosphere. Heat, light, electricity, radio, and x-rays are all known to be energy in the form of transverse vibrations. Physically, they differ only in their wave lengths, but their physical effects are quite different, as is evident by comparing heat with radio waves. In radiation, nothing but energy really travels.

Radiation does not heat the air through which it passes, it heats only the objects on which it falls. Not only the sun, but other objects such as flames, stoves, electric light bulbs, machines, and the earth itself, radiate heat. Even our bodies radiate heat.

H3. **Convection.**—Convection is the transfer of heat by the movement of a substance (gas or liquid) through a space. Examples of this include a current of warm air in a room, a current of warm water such as the Gulf Stream, and warm air rising from a hot water or steam radiator.

H4. **Conduction.**—The transfer of heat from one molecule to another, either of the same substance or of different substances, by direct contact is called conduction. A molecule of a substance is the smallest particle of a substance that retains the special qualities of that substance. Any further subdivision of a molecule separates it into the atoms of which it is composed.

Physical contact is necessary for conduction of heat, and the conduction takes place from the region of the higher temperature to the lower temperature. For example, if a person holds a metal bar of iron in one hand and places the other end of the bar in a fire, the heat passes from the fire to the bar, then along the bar to the hand. Here physical contact is made in each instance; fire to bar, bar to hand.

H5. **Thermal Conductance.**—Suppose that two bars are held, one of iron and one of copper, of exactly the same size and at the same temperature. If one end of each bar is placed in a fire at the same time, heat will reach the hand holding the copper bar more quickly than through the iron bar. This is because some substances conduct heat more readily than others.

This characteristic of a substance is called its thermal or heat conductance. The low and high thermal conductance of substances is of great importance in refrigeration and air conditioning. Some substances are used for transfer of heat while others are used to prevent heat transfer.

## I. INSULATION

**I1. Need for Insulation.**—It is comparatively easy to heat or cool articles or enclosed spaces. It is not easy, however, to keep them at a constant temperature because heat constantly tends to flow to the lower temperature areas.

When it is desired to keep a space within a certain temperature range, it is necessary to prevent the transfer of heat to or from the space. Fortunately this can be done, fairly successfully, by the use of a substance with low thermal conductance.

**I2. Insulators.**—Poor conductors are good insulators. Poor conductors include such substances as cork, wood, sawdust, paper, brick, rubber, fur, feathers, felt, plastics, cotton, and dead air space. Most solids that are poor conductors are also porous in nature, and the pores or air cells are small in size. Much of the insulating quality results from these tiny pockets.

The "K" conductivity factor for an insulating material is the amount of Btu per square foot, per hour, per °F, that can penetrate the insulation for a thickness of one inch. Some of the more commonly used insulating materials and "K" conductivity factors follow:

| Material | "K" Factor |
|---|---|
| Cork with pitch | 0.428 |
| Sawdust, pine | 0.57 |
| Wool, pure | 0.26 |
| Glass | 5.0 |
| Air (dead) | 0.175 |

**I3. Low Temperature Insulation.**—The requirements for low-temperature insulation are somewhat different from those for high-temperature insulation. Any water vapor present in the air tends to condense into liquid droplets or film on a cold surface. This is commonly called sweating. This condensed water penetrates a porous material and fills the air cells, lessening its insulating ability. It may freeze there and ice is a very poor insulator of heat. Insulating materials for use with refrigeration systems are manufactured to resist the penetration of moisture, and to be durable under conditions of high humidity.

Low-temperature pipe lines must be thoroughly insulated to prevent heat from entering the refrigerant contained therein. The usual insulation is a cork composition molded into sections that fit snugly around the pipes and fittings. Other materials, such as rock wool and mineral wool, are also used in the same way.

Before applying the covering, all pipes should be carefully cleaned, all rust removed, and dried. If possible, the hangers and braces should be attached around the outside of the insulation to prevent the transfer of heat by conduction and to prevent moisture from entering the insulation.

When molded sections are installed on pipe lines, they should be staggered and all joints should be placed so as to come together at the top and bottom of the pipe. After all seams are sealed, the covering should be painted with an asphalt paint, to make it waterproof.

Always repair ruptured insulation as soon as possible to prevent the entry of moisture. Make sure the pipe is dry and all seams are sealed when making repairs.

# BASIC FUNDAMENTALS OF AIR CONDITIONING AND REFRIGERATION

## TABLE OF CONTENTS

| | Page |
|---|---|
| I. Operation | 1 |
|    A. Using the Dehydrator | 1 |
|    B. V-Belt Drive | 1 |
|    C. Checking Compressor Oil | 2 |
| II. Maintenance | 3 |
|    A. Compressor Maintenance | 3 |
|    B. Removing Shaft Seal | 5 |
|    C. Installing Shaft Seal | 5 |
|    D. Lapping Shaft Seal | 6 |
| III. System Maintenance | 6 |
|    A. Charging the System | 6 |
|    B. Purging Air from the System | 7 |
|    C. Cleaning Suction Strainers | 7 |
|    D. Cleaning Liquid Line Strainer | 7 |
|    E. Cleaning Oil Filters and Strainers | 7 |
| IV. Condensers | 8 |
|    A. Checking Condenser Performance | 8 |
|    B. Cleaning Condenser Tubes | 8 |
|    C. Cleaning Air-Cooled Condensers | 9 |
|    D. Testing for Leaks | 9 |
|    E. Retubing Condensers | 9 |
| V. Expansion Valves | 10 |
|    A. Thermostatic Expansion Valve | 10 |
|    B. Automatic Expansion Valve | 12 |
|    C. Hand Expansion Valve | 13 |
|    D. Switches | 13 |
|    E. Evacuating and Dehydrating the System | 13 |
|    F. Reactivating the Drying System | 14 |
|    G. Cleaning the System | 16 |
| VI. Detecting and Correcting Troubles | 16 |
|    A. Trouble-Diagnosis Chart | 17 |

# BASIC FUNDAMENTALS OF AIR CONDITIONING AND REFRIGERATION

I. OPERATION

Proper operation of any unit of machinery is an important part of maintaining it. To ensure proper operation of the refrigeration plant, it is necessary to understand the principles of operation of the unit. It is also necessary to make periodic inspections and tests. It is good practice to make an hourly check of all temperatures and pressures throughout the system and to check the oil level in the compressor crankcase.

One of the best methods, and probably the easiest, for checking plant operation is to compare the temperatures and pressures of the plant with corresponding temperatures and pressures which were recorded during a period when the plant was known to be operating properly. The value of the comparison will depend on the similarity of the conditions existing when each set of readings was taken.

A daily operating log for refrigeration equipment should be maintained and used for a continuous analysis of the operating conditions found in a refrigeration plant.

Refrigeration plants are equipped with automatic controls and once the plant is in normal operation, very little attention is required. However, these plants are, like all units of machinery, liable to casualties, so periodic checks must be made to ensure that the plant is operating normally. The main purpose of the operating log is to ensure that abnormal operating conditions do not go undetected.

Usually the personnel assigned to operate and maintain refrigeration plants are graduates of an air conditioning and refrigeration school. However, in small shops, the men assigned to make the periodic checks on the refrigeration plants may or may not have attended this school. These men must be properly indoctrinated as to how to take and record the temperatures and pressures in a refrigeration plant and also as to why these readings are important for the operation of the plant.

A. USING THE DEHYDRATOR

A dehydrator is installed in the liquid line between the receiver and the expansion valve to absorb moisture that has entered the system. The dehydrator is installed with a bypass so that it may be cut in or out of the system. The dehydrator should be put into use when the system is being charged, at any time the system is opened for repairs, or at any time the presence of moisture is suspected.

Dehydrators can absorb only small quantities of moisture and are installed to minimize the effects of moisture. If large quantities of moisture are present in the refrigeration system, more than one dehydrator must be used, or other means must be taken to rid the system of moisture. Another drying-out process is described in this chapter under "Evacuating and Dehydrating the System."

B. V-BELT DRIVE

Belts must be properly tightened. Excessive looseness will cause slippage, rapid wear, and deterioration of V-belts. On the other hand, a belt that is too tight will result in excessive wear of both the belt and main bearing of the compressor. In extreme cases, it may cause a bad seal leak. If a belt is properly tightened, it should be possible to depress it, by the pressure of one finger, as much as 1/2 to 3/4 inch, at a point midway between the flywheel and motor pulleys.

When replacement of one belt of a multiple V-belt drive is necessary, a complete new set of matched belts should be installed. Belts stretch considerably during the first few hours of operation. Replacement of a single belt will upset the load balance between the new and old belts and be a potential source of trouble. It is better practice to run the unit temporarily with a defective belt removed than to attempt to operate a new belt in conjunction with two or more seasoned belts.

V-belts, motor pulleys, and compressor flywheels should be kept dry and free of oil. Belt dressing should never be used.

### C. CHECKING COMPRESSOR OIL

If the apparent oil level observed immediately after a prolonged shutdown period is lower than normal, it is almost certain that the actual working oil level is far too low. After a sufficient quantity of oil has been added to raise the apparent oil level to the center of the bull's-eye sight glass, on the side of the compressor, the actual oil level should be checked as follows:

1. Operate the compressor or manual control for at least one hour. Then slowly close the suction line stop valve. If the compressor is operating on a water cooler or other coil which is apt to freeze, observe the temperature and interrupt compressor operation as necessary to prevent freezing. Repeat cycling until the total running time (one hour) is obtained.

2. Stop the compressor, turn the flywheel until the crankshaft and connecting rod ends are immersed in the lubricating oil, and immediately observe the oil level in the sight glass.

To check the oil level when the compressor has been running on its normal cycle, with no abnormal shutdown, proceed as follows:

1. Wait until the end of a period of operation; if the operation is continuous, wait until the compressor has been in operation at least 1/2 hour.

2. As soon as the compressor stops, turn the flywheel until the crankshaft and connecting rod ends are immersed in the lubricating oil, and observe the oil level in the sight glass.

Do not remove oil from the crankcase because of an apparent high level unless it is known that too much oil has been previously added, or unless it is apparent that oil from the crankcase of one compressor of the plant has been inadvertently deposited in the crankcase of another.

However, if the oil level is lower than its recommended height on the glass, additional oil should be added. Do not add more oil than is necessary to obtain the desired level. Too much oil can result in excessive oil transfer to the cooling coils.

Adding Oil

There are two common methods of adding oil to a compressor. In one type of installation a small oil-charging pump is furnished for adding oil to the compressor crankcase. In another type, oil is placed in the compressor by means of a clean, well-dried funnel. In either case, care must be taken to prevent the entrance of air or foreign matter into the compressor.

When performing hourly checks of the compressors, you may observe no oil in the crank-case, or a very low oil level on the sight glass. This indicates that the oil has left the compressor and is circulating in the system; and that it will be necessary to add oil to the normal level and operate the system. After the compressor has reclaimed the excessive oil in the system, the added oil should be drained.

Removing Oil

To remove oil from the compressor crank-case, reduce the pressure in the crankcase to approximately 1 psi by gradually closing the suction line stop valve. Then stop the compressor, close the suction and discharge line valves, loosen the lubricating oil drain plug near the bottom of the compressor crankcase, and allow the required amount of oil to drain out. Since the compressor crankcase is under a slight pressure, do not fully remove the drain plug from the compressor, but allow the oil to seep out around the threads of the loosened plug.

When the desired amount of oil has been removed, tighten the drain plug, open the suction and discharge line valves, and start the compressor. If an oil drain valve is provided in lieu of a plug, the required amount of oil may be drained without the necessity of pumping down the compressor.

Changing Oil

When clean copper tubing is employed for the mains and evaporators, and reasonable care has been taken to prevent the entrance of foreign matter during installation, the oil in the compressor crankcase will probably not become sufficiently contaminated to require renewal. When iron or steel pipe and fittings are used in the system, a sample of oil from the compressor crankcase should be withdrawn into a clean glass vessel every three months. If the sample shows contamination, the entire lubricating oil charge should be renewed. It is good practice to check the cleanliness of the lubricating oil after each cleaning of the compressor suction scale trap.

## II. MAINTENANCE

In order for you to perform the required maintenance you must understand the proper operating and maintenance procedures. In most instances, personnel who are assigned to maintain refrigeration plants are graduates of an Air Conditioning and

Refrigeration School. While this school teaches most operating and maintenance procedures, the manufacturer's technical manuals should be referred to for the details of the plants on your ship.

### A. COMPRESSOR MAINTENANCE

Refrigeration compressors vary to such an extent that this training course could not cover each type. The manufacturer's technical manuals must be referred to for details of any specific unit. Compressors range from small reciprocating types (for drinking water coolers) to very large centrifugal units used for air conditioning on large ships. Compressors may be splash lubricated or forced-feed lubricated. Centrifugal compressors are seldom used on plants smaller than 110 tons. They operate on the same principle as a centrifugal pump, except that they are designed to pump a gas instead of a liquid. Reciprocating compressors are used for air conditioning on most ships.

If a compressor cannot be pumped down and is damaged to the extent that it has to be opened fox repairs, it is necessary to first close the suction and discharge valves and then allow all refrigerant in the compressor to vent to the atmosphere, through a gage line.

To service a compressor correctly, it is necessary to be familiar with the manufacturer's technical manual. These manuals usually give a step-by-step procedure for disassembling the compressor and for renewing any part of the unit.

Before disassembling a compressor, make certain that the faulty operation of the unit is not caused by trouble in some other part of the system. Disassemble only the part of the compressor that is necessary to correct the fault. As internal machined parts are removed, every precaution should be taken to protect them from being damaged in handling and from corrosion.

Before starting to reassemble a compressor, all partsincluding replacement parts should be carefully washed in an approved solvent and permitted to dry in air. The final rinse should be made with clean solvent. The parts should be wiped with a lintfree cloth before the unit is assembled. Every precaution should betaken to prevent dirt, lint, water, or other foreign matter from entering the compressor during reassembly.

When it becomes necessary to remove, replace, or repair internal parts of the compressor, the following precautions should be observed:

1. Carefully disassemble and remove parts, noting the correct relative position so that errors will not be made when reassembling.

2. Inspect all those parts that become accessible due to the removal of other parts requiring repair or replacement.

3. Make certain that all parts and surfaces are free of dirt and moisture.

4. Apply compressor oil freely to all bearing and rubbing surfaces of parts being replaced or reinstalled.

5. If the compressor is not equipped with an oil pump, make certain the oil dipper on the lower connecting rod is in correct position for dipping oil when the unit is in operation.

6. Position the ends of the piston rings so that alternate joints come on the opposite side of the piston.

7. Care should be taken not to score gasket surfaces.

8. Renew all gaskets.

9. Clean the crankcase and renew the oil.

Whenever repairs to a compressor are of such a nature that any appreciable amount of air enters the unit, the compressor should be evacuated, after assembly is completed. The proper procedure is as follows:

1. Disconnect a connection in the compressor discharge gage line, between the discharge line stop valve and the compressor.

2. Start the compressor and let it run until the greatest possible vacuum is obtained.

3. Stop the compressor and immediately open the suction stop valve slightly in order to blow refrigerant through the compressor valves and purge the air above the discharge valves through the open gage line.

4. Close the discharge gage line and open the discharge line stop valve.

5. Remove all oil from the exterior of the compressor, and test the compressor joints for leakage, using the halide leak detector.

Testing Suction and Discharge Valves

A compressor should not be opened for inspection or repair until it has definitely been determined that the faulty operation of the system is or is not due to leaky suction or discharge valves.

Faulty compressor valves may be indicated either by a gradual or a sudden decrease in the normal compressor capacity. Either the compressor will fail to pump at all, or else the suction pressure cannot be pumped down to the designed value, and the compressor will run for abnormally long intervals or even continuously. If the compressor shuts down for short periods, the compressor valves may be leaking.

If the refrigeration plant is not operating satisfactorily, it will be best to first shift the compressors and then check the operation of the plant. If the operation of the plant is still not satisfactory when the compressors have been shifted, the trouble is in the system, and not in the compressor.

The compressor discharge valves may be tested by pumping down the compressor to 2 psig, and then stopping the compressor and quickly closing the suction and discharge line valves. If the discharge pressure drops at a rate in excess of 3 pounds in a minute and the crankcase suction pressure rises, there is evidence of compressor discharge valve leakage. If it is necessary to remove the discharge valves with the compressor pumped down, open the connection to the discharge pressure gage in order to release discharge pressure on the head. Then remove the compressor top head and discharge valve plate, being careful not to damage the gaskets.

If the discharge valves are defective, the entire discharge valve assembly should be replaced. Any attempt to repair them would probably involve relapping, and would require highly specialized equipment. Except in an emergency, such repair should never be undertaken aboard ship.

The compressor internal suction valves may be checked for leakage as follows:

1. Start the compressor by using the manual control switch on the motor controller.

2. Close the suction line stop valve gradually, to prevent violent foaming of the compressor crankcase lubricating oil charge.

3. With this stop valve closed, pump a vacuum of approximately 20 inches Hg. If this vacuum can be readily obtained, the compressor suction valves are satisfactory.

Do not expect the vacuum to be maintained after the compressor stops, because the Refrigerant-12 is being released from the crankcase oil. Do not attempt to check compressor suction valve efficiency of new units until after the compressor has been in operation for a minimum of 3 days. It may be necessary for the valves to wear in.

However, if any of the compressor suction valves are defective, the compressor should be pumped down, opened, and the valves inspected. Defective valve(s) or pistons should be replaced with spare assemblies.

Crankshaft Seal Repairs

On reciprocating compressors, the crankshaft extends through the compressor housing to provide a mount for the pulley wheel. At this point the shaft must be sealed to prevent leakage of lubricating oil and refrigerant. There are several types of crankshaft seals, depending on the manufacturer. The crankshaft seal is bathed in lubricating oil at a pressure equal to the suction pressure of the refrigerant. The first indication of crankshaft failure is excessive oil leaking at the shaft.

When the seal requires replacement, or signs of abnormal wear or damage to the running surfaces are present, a definite reason for the abnormal conditions exists and an inspection should be made. It is very important to locate and correct the trouble or the failure will reoccur.

Seal failure is very often the result of faulty lubrication, usually due to the condition of the crankcase oil. Dirty or broken oil is generally caused by one or both of the following conditions:

1. Dirt or foreign material in the system or system piping. Dirt frequently enters the system at the time of installation. After a period of operation, foreign mate rial will always accumulate in the compressor crankcase, tending to concentrate in the oil chamber surrounding the shaft seal. When the oil contains grit, it is only a matter of time until the highly finished running faces become damaged, causing failure of the shaft seal.

2. Moisture is frequently the cause of an acid condition of the lubricating oil. Oil in this condition will not provide satisfactory lubrication and will promote failure of the compressor parts. If the presence of moisture is suspected, a dryer should be used when the compressor is put into operation. At any time foreign mate rial is found in the lubricating oil, the entire system (piping, valves, and strainers) should be cleaned thoroughly.

B. REMOVING SHAFT SEAL.— In the event a shaft seal must be repaired or renewed, proceed as follows:

If the seal is broken to the extent that it permits excessive oil leakage, do not attempt to pump the refrigerant out of the compressor, air (containing moisture) will be drawn into the system through the damaged seal. Moisture in the air may cause expansion valves to freeze. If oil is leaking excessively, close the compressor suction and discharge valves and relieve the pressure to the atmosphere by loosening a connection on the compressor discharge gage line. If the condition of the seal does permit, pump down the compressor as previously explained in this chapter.

Next drain the oil from the compressor crankcase. Since the oil contains refrigerant, it will foam while being drained. The oil drain valve or plug should be left open while you are working on the seal, so that refrigerant escaping from the oil remaining in the crankcase will not build up a pressureand unexpectedly blow out the seal while it is being removed.

Remove the compressor flywheel (or coupling) and carefully remove the shaft seal assembly. If the assembly cannot be readily removed, build up a slight pressure in the compressor crankcase by slightly opening the compressor suction valve, taking the necessary precautions to support the seal to prevent it from being blown from the compressor and damaged.

C. INSTALLING SHAFT SEAL.— When the replacement is made, the entire seal assembly should be replaced. The parts should be clean and should be replaced in accordance with the manufacturer's instructions.

Wipe the shaft clean with a linen or silk cloth, do not use a dirty or lint-bearing cloth. Unwrap the seal, being careful not to touch the bearing surfaces with the hands. Rinse the seal in an approved solvent and allow to air-dry. (Do not wipe the seal dry.) Dip the seal in clean refrigerant oil. Insert the assembly in accordance with the instructions found in the manufacturer's technical manual and bolt the seal cover in place, tightening the bolts evenly. Replace the flywheel and belts and test the unit for leaks by opening the suction and discharge valves and using a halide leak detector.

D. LAPPING SHAFT SEAL.— Due to the difficulty of properly lapping the rubbing surfaces of a shaft seal, a seal leak should be corrected by renewing the assembly. If, however, a new shaft seal is not available, and it is possible to use the existing seal by refinishingthe rubbing surfaces, the seal can be lapped as follows:

1. Thoroughly clean the surfaces of the shaft shoulder and seal collar.

2. Lap the back of the shaft seal collar to the crankshaft shoulder. This joint must form an absolute seal so the importance of this lapping cannot be overemphasized. Only jeweler's rouge or the equivalent should be used for the lapping. The abrasive must be used sparingly to avoid getting it into the shaft bearings or crankcase. As the lapping proceeds, use less and less abrasive and finish the lapping with compressor lubricating Oil.

3. After the lapping has been completed, thoroughly clean the shaft shoulder and permit it to dry without wiping. With the shaft seal shoulder and collar dry and clean, lap the two surfaces together as a final lapping operation.

4. The surfaces are properly lapped when the surface of both the shaft shoulder and the shaft seal collar form a perfect contact and are free of all mars, scratches, or other imperfections.  It is good practice to make the final examination with the aid of a good magnifying glass.

5. In some instances, a molded synthetic rubber gasket is provided instead of the metal-to-metal joint between the shaft seal collar and the crankshaft shoulder. In any case, it is extremely important that these parts be properly fitted and that the gasket be kept in good condition in order that a tight seal be maintained at this point.

When a shaft seal is lapped in, it should be regarded as a temporary repair and a new assembly should be installed as soon as possible.

III. SYSTEM MAINTENANCE

A refrigeration system that has been properly installed and properly operated will need little maintenance. However, certain tests, inspections, and maintenance procedures must be carried out to ensure that the system will operate at its rated capacity.

Learning to start and secure a refrigeration system is not enough to do your job properly. As a mechanic you must know the operating principles of the entire system, how each unit of the system operates, and why it is necessary; how each control and safety device works, and the reason for its being installed on the system. This understanding can be attained only through study, either by attending an Air Conditioning and Refrigeration School or by studying the manufacturer's technical manuals.

For men who have not attended an Air Conditioning and Refrigeration School, a training program should be set up to ensure an adequate number of qualified personnel to operate and maintain the air conditioning and refrigeration equipment.

A. Charging the System

Information concerning the charging of refrigeration systems mav be found in a technical manual. The amount of refrigerant charge must be sufficient to maintain a liquid seal between the condensing and evaporating sides of the system. When the compressor stops, under normal operating conditions, the receiver of a properly charged system is about 85 percent full of refrigerant. The proper charge for a specific system or unit can be found in the manufacturer's technical manual or on the blueprints.

A refrigeration system should not be charged if there are leaks or if there is reason to believe that thereisaleakinthe system. The leaks must be found and corrected. Immediately following or duringthe process of charging, the system should be carefully checked for leaks.

A refrigeration system must have an adequate charge of refrigerant at all times; otherwise its efficiency and capacity will be impaired.

B.   Purging Air From The System

Operate the system for 30 minutes. Observe the pressure and temperature as indicated on the high pressure gage. Read the thermometer in the liquid line, and compare it with the temperature conversion figures shown on the discharge pressure gage. If the temperature of the liquid leaving the receiver is more than 15° F lower than the temperature corresponding to the discharge pressure, the system should be purged. While the system is still operating, slightly open the purge valve on the condenser. Purge very slowly, at intervals, until the air is expelled from the system and the temperature difference drops below 15° F.

C.   Cleaning Suction Strainers

When putting a new unit into operation, the suction strainers should be cleaned after a few hours of operation. Refrigerants have a solvent action and will loosen any foreign matter in the system. This foreign matter will eventually reach the suction strainers. After a few days of operation, the strainers will need another cleaning. They should be inspected frequently during the first few weeks of plant operation, and then cleaned as found necessary.

The suction strainers are located in the compressor housing or in the suction piping. The procedure for cleaning the strainers is as follows:

   1.   Pump down the compressor.
   2.   Remove the strainer and inspect it for foreign matter.
   3.   Clean the strainer screen by dipping it in an approved solvent and then allow it to dry.
   4.   Replace the strainer and evacuate the air from the compressor.
   5.   Test the housing for leaks by wiping up all oil and then using a halide leak detector.

D.   Cleaning A Liquid Line Strainer

Where a liquid line strainer is installed, it should be cleaned at the same intervals as the suction strainer. If a liquid line strainer becomes clogged to the extent that it needs cleaning, a loss of refrigeration effect will take place. The tubing after the strainer will be much colder than the tubing ahead of the strainer.

To clean the liquid line strainer, secure the receiver outlet valve and wait a few minutes to allow any liquid in the strainer to flow to the cooling coils. Then close the strainer outlet valve and very carefully loosen the cap which is bolted to the strainer body. (Use goggles to protect the eyes.) When all of the pressure is bled out of the strainer, remove the cap and lift out the strainer screen. Clean the strainer screen, using an approved solvent and a small brush. Reassemble the spring and screen in the strainer body, then replace the strainer cap loosely. Purge the air out of the strainer, by blowing refrigerant through it, then tighten the cap. After the assembly is complete, test the unit for leaks.

E.   Cleaning Oil Filters and Strainers

Compressors arranged for forced feed lubri-' cation are provided with lubricating oil strainers in the suction line of the lube oil pump and an oil filter may be installed in the pump discharge line. A gradual decrease in lubricating oil pressure indicates that these units need cleaning. This cleaning may be accomplished in much the same manner as described for cleaning suction strainers.

When cleaning is necessary, the lubricating oil in the crankcase should be drained from the compressor and a new charge of oil should be added before restarting the unit.

When the compressor is put back into operation, the lube oil pressure should be adjusted to the proper setting by adjustment of the oil pressure regulator.

## IV. CONDENSERS

The compressor discharge line terminates at the refrigerant condenser. In shipboard R-12 installations, these condensers are usually of the multipass shell-and-tube type, with water circulating through the tubes. The tubes are expanded into grooved holes in the tube sheet so as to make an absolutely tight joint between the shell and the circulating water. Refrigerant vapor is admitted to the shell, and condenses on the outer surfaces of the tubes.

Any air which may accidentally enter the refrigeration system will be drawn through the piping and eventually discharged into the condenser with the R-12 gas. The air accumulated in the condenser is lighter than the refrigerant gas and will rise to the top of the condenser when the plant is shut down. A purge valve, for purging accumulated air from the refrigeration system (when necessary), is installed at the top of the condenser, or at a high point in the compressor discharge line.

### A. Checking Condenser Performance

An overall check for water-cooled condenser performance may be used after, AND ONLY AFTER, the condenser has been properly purged. After the condition of the condensing surface has been determined, make preliminary preparations to the system as outlined in the procedure, discussed earlier in the chapter, used to check for noncondensable gases. Then proceed as follows:

1. Record the condensing temperature which corresponds to the pressure in the condenser, while the compressor is in operation.
2. Record the temperature of the water leaving the condenser.
3. Subtract the temperature of the water leaving the condenser from the condensing temperature obtained in (1). The temperature of the water leaving the condenser will be several degrees below the condensing temperature of pure R-12.
4. Clean the water side of the condenser, if the difference between the temperature of the outlet circulating water and the temperature corresponding to the condensing pressure increases 5° F to 10° F above the temperature difference obtained when the condenser was in good condition and operating under similar heat loads, and if this difference is not caused by an overcharge of refrigerant or noncondensable gases.

### B. Cleaning Condenser Tubes

In order to clean the condenser tubes properly, it is necessary first to drain the cooling water from the condenser and then to remove the water connections and water chests. When the water chests are removed, be careful not to damage the gaskets between the tube sheet and the water side of the water chest. Tubes should be inspected as often as practicable and be cleaned as necessary by the use of an approved method for cleaning steam condenser tubes.

Rubber plugs and an air or water lance should be employed when necessary to remove foreign deposits. It is essential that the tube surfaces be kept clear of particles of foreign matter; however, care must be taken not to destroy the thin protective coating of corrosion products on the inner surfaces of the tubes. If the tubes become badly corroded, they should be replaced in order to avoid the possibility of losing the R-12 charge and admitting salt water to the R-12 system.

C.  Cleaning Air-Cooled Condensers

Although the large plants are equipped with water-cooled condensers, auxiliary units are commonly provided with air-cooled condensers, and this eliminates the necessity for circulating water pumps and piping.

The exterior surface of the tubes and fins on an air-cooled condenser should be kept free of dirt or any matter that might obstruct heat flow and air circulation. The finned surface should be brushed clean with a stiff bristle brush as often as necessary. When installations are exposed to salt spray and rain through open doors or hatches, care should be taken to minimize corrosion of the exterior surfaces. The finned surface is usually coated with solder and should never be painted; it may be retinned if necessary.

D.  Testing for Leaks

To prevent serious loss of refrigerant through leaky condenser tubes, the condenser should be tested for leakage once every two weeks. The test should always be conducted on a condenser that has not been in use for the preceding 12 hours. Slowly open the vent valves on the water side, one at a time, and insert the exploring tube of a leak detector. If this test indicates that R-12 gas is present, the exact location of the leak may be detected by the following method:

1. Remove the water heads and listen at each section for the hissing sound that indicates gas leakage. If the leak cannot be definitely located, all the, tubes must be checked. However, if the probable location of the leaky tubes is found, treat that section as follows:

2. Wash the tube heads, and with a cloth or ball of cotton clean all tubes (while wet) until the inner walls are dry and shining. Then hold the exploring tube in one end of each condenser tube for about 10 seconds. As soon as fresh air is drawn into the tube, drive a cork into each end of the tube. If necessary, repeat this procedure with all the tubes in the condenser. Before proceeding further, allow the condenser to remain in this condition for 48 hours.

3. After the tubes have been corked up for 48 hours, put three men on the job, one to remove corks at one end, another to remove corks at the other end and handle the exploring tube, and the third man to watch the color of the flame in the lamp. Start with the top row of tubes in the section being inspected, remove the corks simultaneously at each end of the tube, and insert the exploring tube for 5 seconds.

4. Mark any leaky tubes for later identification.

5. Leakage of any of the tube joints is indicated by the presence of oil at the joint, after the 48-hour period.

To date, this procedure has been found to be the only method which gives conclusive evidence; in most cases, this method has given satisfactory results.

E.  Retubing Condensers

The general procedure for retubing condensers has been outlined in chapter 6 of this training course. One specific illustration of retubing a refrigerant condenser is as follows:

1. Drill into both ends of the faulty tube or tubes, with a 19/32-inch drill, to a depth of 1/16 inch less than the actual thickness of the tube sheet.

2. Insert the condenser knockout bar. Then insert, in the other end of the tube, a bar 1/2 inch x 6 inches.

3. Proceed to the other end of the condenser and drive out the faulty tube by using the knockout bar.

4. Follow the above procedure for any further tube removal.

5. Cut the new tube 1/8 inch longer than the overall length of the condenser (heads removed).

6. Both ends of the tubes must be square and all inside and outside burrs removed.

7. Insert the new tube in the condenser, leaving 1/16 of an inch protruding from each end.

8. Secure the spacing bar over one end of the tube.

9. Oil the rolling tool, insert it in the tube, and roll the tube into serrations.

10. Remove the spacing bar and roll that end of the tube by the above method.

11. Insert the belling tool and keep rotating while belling. Do not strike too hard on the belling tool.

12. After belling both ends of the tube, grind off the ends flush with the tube sheet.

13. Open the discharge line valve into the condenser, and open any other valves necessary to get gas from the compressor into the condenser.

14. Using the pressure thus obtained, test the condenser for leaks, with the halide torch.

15. If any small leaks exist, reroll the leaking tube. (Spacers are used on the rolling tool to prevent the use of maximum rolling effect on a preliminary rolling operation. Additional rolling effect may be obtained by removing one of these spacers.)

16. Reassemble the condenser.

## V. EXPANSION VALVES

In order to diagnose troubles in a refrigeration plant, it is essential that the mechanic ' have a thorough understanding of the principles and ope ration of expansion valves.

A. Thermostatic Expansion Valve

FUNCTION.– The thermostatic expansion valve controls the quantity of refrigerant admitted to the cooling coil and reduces the pressure of this refrigerant to that pressure maintained in the coil. The valve also operates to feed into the coil the amount of refrigerant necessary to keep the coil working at maximum effectiveness and in accordance with heat load variation, and to prevent the flooding back of liquid refrigerant to the compressor.

OPERATION. – It is apparent that, if the suction gas leaving the cooling coil is at the saturated vapor temperature of the refrigerant and the R-12 in the control bulb is also at this temperature, the control bulb pressure transmitted to the top of the valve diaphragm will be equal to the suction pressure transmitted to the lower side of the diaphragm through the equalizing line. The valve needle will be in the closed position, because of upward pressure exerted by the valve spring. The continued operation of the compressor maintains or lowers the cooling coil suction pressure, but since the valve is closed and no liquid refrigerant is supplied to the coil, the temperature of the coil rises because of the heat absorbed from the space being cooled. The R-12 in the control bulb is in turn heated; and its pressure increases to maintain a saturated pressure corresponding to the cooling coil suction gas temperature. The pressure on top of the power element diaphragm increases, overcomes the spring pressure, and causes the valve needle to open, thus permitting the flow of refrigerant liquid into the coil.

The liquid refrigerant is evaporated during its passage through the coil. Upon leaving the outlet end, the cold vapor cools the R-12 in the control bulb and decreases the upper diaphragm pressure, tending to close the valve. This reduction in valve opening reduces the quantity of refrigerant fed to the cooling coil and permits evaporation of all the liquid before the refrigerant reaches the outlet end where the control bulb is located. The refrigerant vapor becomes superheated during its passage through that part of the coil beyond the point where all liquid is evaporated.

The amount of superheat depends on the valve spring pressure exerted on the diaphragm. For a given spring setting, the valve maintains a relatively constant degree of superheat at the coil outlet, ensuring that all R-12 liquid is evaporated before it leaves the coil to return to the compressor.

EXTERNAL EQUALIZER. – The external equalizing connection is provided for relatively large cooling coil installations where a considerable pressure loss may be expected to occur because of the length of coil travel or the distribution method. This equalizing line is connected to the cooling coil at a convenient point where the desired operating pressures will be reflected. practically equal to that at the coil outlet where the control bulb is located; in such an installation the external equalizing line is unnecessary. Instead, the expansion valve is provided with an internal equalizing port, to adjust the pressure on the lower side of the diaphragm so that it will equal the pressure at the valve outlet.

For small installations the pressure drop through the coil is correspondingly small, and the refrigerant pressure at the valve outlet.

TESTING AND ADJUSTMENT. When the thermostatic expansion valve is operating properly, the temperature at the outlet side of the valve is much lower than that at the inlet side. If this temperature difference does not exist when the system is in operation, the valve seat is probably dirty and clogged with foreign matter.

Once a valve is properly adjusted, further adjustment should not be necessary. The major trouble encountered can usually be traced to moisture or dirt collecting at the valve seat and orifice.

By means of a gear and screw arrangement, the thermostatic expansion valve is adjusted to maintain a superheat ranging approximately from $4°$ F to $12°$ F at the cooling coil outlet. The proper superheat adjustment varies with the design and service operating conditions of the valve, and the design of the particular plant. Increased spring pressure increases the degree of superheat at the coil outlet and decreased pressure has the opposite effect. Many thermostatic expansion valves are initially adjusted by the manufacturer to maintain a predetermined degree of superheat, and no provision is made for further adjustments in service.

If expansion valves are adjusted to give a high degree of superheat at the coil outlet, or if the valve is stuck shut, the amount of refrigerant admitted to the cooling coil will be reduced. With an insufficient amount of refrigerant, the coil will be "starved" and will operate at a reduced capacity. Compressor lubricating oil carried with the refrigerant may tend to collect at the bottom of the cooling coils, thus robbing the compressor crankcase, and providing a condition whereby slugs of lubricating oil may be drawn back to the compressor. If the expansion valve is adjusted for too low a degree of superheat, or if the valve is stuck open, liquid refrigerant may flood from the cooling coils back to the compressor. Should the liquid collect at a low point in the suction line or coil, and be drawn back to the compressor intermittently in slugs, there

is danger of injury to the moving parts of the compressor.

In general, the expansion valves for air conditioning and water cooling plants (high temperature installations) must be adjusted for higher superheat than are the expansion valves for cold storage refrigeration and ship's service store equipment (low temperature installations).

If it is impossible to adjust expansion valves to the desired settings, or if it is suspected that the expansion valve assembly is defective and requires replacement, appropriate tests must be made. (First be sure that the liquid strainers are clean, that the solenoid valves are operative, and that the system is sufficiently charged with refrigerant.)

The major equipment required for expansion valve tests is as follows:

1. A service drum of R-12, or a supply of clean dry air at 70 to 100 psig. The service drum is used to supply gas under pressure. The gas used does not have to be the same as that employed in the thermal element of the valve being tested.

2. A high pressure and a low pressure gage. The low pressure gage should be accurate and in good condition so that the pointer does not have any appreciable lost motion. The high pressure gage, while not absolutely necessary, will be useful in showing the pressure on the inlet side of the valve. Refrigeration plants are provided with suitable spare and test pressure gages.

The procedure for testing is as follows:

1. Connect the valve inlet to the gas supply with the high pressure gage attached so as to indicate the gas pressure to the valve, and with the low pressure gage loosely connected to the expansion valve outlet. The low pressure gage is connected up loosely so as to provide a small amount of leakage through the connection.

2. Insert the expansion valve thermal element in a bath of crushed ice. Do not attempt to perform this test with a container full of water in which a small amount of crushed ice is floating.

3. Open the valve on the service drum or in the air supply line. Make certain that the gas supply is sufficient to build up the pressure to at least 70 psi on the high pressure gage connected in the line to the valve inlet.

4. The expansion valve can now be adjusted. If it is desired to adjust for 10° F superheat, the pressure on the outlet gage should be 22.5 psig. This is equivalent to an R-12 evaporating temperature of 22° F, and since the ice maintains the bulb at 32° F, the valve adjustment is for 10 superheat (difference between 32 and 22). For a 5 superheat adjustment, the valve should be adjusted to give a pressure of approximately 26.1 psig. There must be a small .amount of leakage through the low pressure gage connection while this adjustment is being made.

5. To determine if the valve operates smoothly, tap the valve body lightly with a small weight. The low pressure gage needle should not jump more than 1 psi.

6. Now tighten the low pressure gage connection so as to stop the leakage at the joint, and determine if the expansion valve seats tightly. With the valve in good condition, the pressure will increase a few pounds and then either stop or build up very slowly. With a leaking valve, the pressure will build up rapidly until it equals the inlet pressure.

7. Again loosen the gage so as to permit leakage at the gage connection; remove the thermal element, or control bulb, from the crushed ice, and warm it with the hand or place it in water that is at room temperature. When this is done, the pressure should increase rapidly, showing that the power element has not lost its charge. If there is no increase in pressure, the power element is dead.

8. With high pressure showing on both gages as outlined above, the valve can be tested to determine if the body joints or the bellows leak. This can be done by using a halide leak detector. When performing this test, it is important that the body of the valve have a fairly high pressure applied to it. In addition, the gages and other fittings should be made up tightly at the joints so as to eliminate leakage at these points.

REPLACEMENT OF VALVE. — If it is evident that the expansion valve is defective, it must be replaced. Often it is possible to replace a faulty power element or other part of the valve without having to replace the entire assembly. When replacement of an expansion valve is necessary, it is important to replace the unit with a valve of the same capacity and type, designed for R-12 systems.

B. Automatic Expansion Valve

Automatic expansion valves are generally similar in construction to thermostatic valves except that the thermostatic element is omitted. The refrigerant pressure in the cooling coil operates on the lower side of the diaphragm and atmospheric pressure operates on the upper side. The amount of valve opening depends upon the pressure existing in the coil. As the operation of the compressor lowers the coil pressure, there is a corresponding decrease in pressure on the lower side of the diaphragm; when this pressure becomes less than the atmospheric pressure on the upper side, the diaphragm is depressed and the valve opens. The pressure at which the valve will open can be predetermined by an adjustment of the valve. As the compressor continues to operate, the needle valve remains open enough to maintain the refrigerant evaporating pressure. When the compressor stops, the coil pressure increases and the valve automatically closes. Thermostatic expansion valves have proved to be more satisfactory than automatic expansion valves for refrigeration plant applications.

C. Hand Expansion Valve

A bypass line equipped with a manually operated expansion valve is installed around the strainer and the cooling coil liquid control valve assembly to permit repair or cleaning. The hand expansion valve is generally similar in design to the other refrigerant stop valves installed in refrigeration systems, except that the valve disk is sometimes specially shaped to permit accurate adjustment of flow. Hand expansion valves should be used only for emergency purposes, since there is the possibility of flooding liquid refrigerant back to the compressor.

D. Switches

In order to trouble-shoot or diagnose switch troubles, it is essential that you have a good understanding of pressurestats and thermostats. A pressurestat is an electric switch actuated by pressure from an outside source. The thermostat is actuated by temperature or heat on a specially prepared thermo-bulb, filled with a substance that expands and contracts with any change in temperature.

A switch that cuts out when there is an increase in pressure or temperature is known as a direct acting switch. When the pressure or temperature is decreased, the switch cuts in. The high pressure switch is a direct acting switch. A reverse acting switch is one that cuts in on an increase of pressure or temperature and cuts out on a decrease of pressure or temperature. The low pressure cutout, thermostat, and water-failure switches are reverse acting switches.

E. Evacuating and Dehydrating the System

Where moisture accumulation must be corrected, the system should first be cleared of refrigerant and air. The time required for these processes will depend upon the size of the system and the amount of moisture present. It is good engineering practice to circulate heated air through a large dehydrator and system for several hours, or as long as the dehydrator drying agent remains effective, before proceeding with the evacuation process. If possible, the dehydrated air should be heated to about $240^\circ$ F.

Large dehydrators, suitable for preliminary dehydration of R-12 systems, are usually available at naval shipyards, and aboard tenders and repair ships.

After the preliminary dehydration, remaining moisture is evacuated by means of a two-stage high-efficiency vacuum pump having a vacuum indicator. (These vacuum pumps are available aboard tenders and repair ships.)

The vacuum indicator shown in figure 10-1 consists of an insulated test tube containing a wet bulb thermometer with its wick immersed in distilled water. The indicator is connected in the vacuum pump suction line. The suction line from the vacuum pump is connected to the charging connection in the refrigeration system. The refrigerant circuit should be closed to the atmosphere and the charging connection opened to the vacuum pump.

A two-stage pump is started for operation in parallel so that maximum displacement may be secured during the initial pump-downstages. When the indicator shows a temperature of about $55^\circ$ F (0.43 inch Hg, absolute), the pumps are placed in series operation (wherein the discharge from the first step enters the suction of the second step pump). The dehydration process will be reflected in the temperature drop of the vacuum indicator, as shown in figure 10-2. Readings will initially reflect ambient temperatures, then show rapidly falling temperatures until the water in the system starts to boil.

When most of the evaporated moisture has been evacuated from the system, the indicator will show a decrease in temperature. When the temperature reaches $35^\circ$ F (0.2 inch Hg, absolute), open the system at a point farthest from the pump; at this point, air should be drawn into the system through a chemical dehydrator, and meanwhile the pump should be operated to permit dilution of moisture present in the system. Close off the opening and re-evacuate until the indicator again shows a temperature of $35^\circ$ F. At this point the dehydration process is complete; close the charging valve and then stop the pump.

Sometimes it will be impossible to obtain a temperature as low as 35° F in the vacuum indicator; the probable reasons for such a failure, and the corrective procedures to take, are as follows:

1. Presence of excess moisture in the system. The dehydration procedure should be conducted for longer periods.

2. Presence of absorbed refrigerant in the lubricating oil contained in the compressor crankcase. Remove the lubricating oil from the crankcase before proceeding with the dehydration process.

3. Leakage of air into the system. The leak must be found and stopped. It will be necessary to repeat the procedure required for detecting leaks in the system.

4. Inefficient vacuum pump or defective vacuum indicator. The defective unit(s) should be repaired or replaced.

F. Reactivating the Drying System

Immediately after each period of use, or after the system has been opened for repairs, the drying agent in the dehydrator should be replaced. If a replacement cartridge is not available, the drying agent can be reactivated and used until a replacement is available.

Reactivation is accomplished by removing the drying agent and heating it, for 12 hours, to a temperature of 300° F to bake out the moisture. The drying agent may be placed in an oven, or a stream of hot air may be circulated through the cartridge. These methods are satisfactory for reactivating commonly used dehydrating agents such as activated alumina and silica gel. Where special drying agents are employed, they should be reactivated in accordance with specific instructions furnished by the manufacturer.

Figure 1.—Dehydrator vacuum indicator.

Figure 2.—Vacuum indicator readings plotted during dehydration.

After reactivation, the drying agent should be replaced in the dehydrator shell and sealed as quickly as possible, in order to prevent absorption of atmospheric moisture. When the drying agent becomes fouled or saturated with lubricating oil, it must be replaced by a fresh spare charge, or dehydrator cartridge, taken from a sealed container.

Remember that the dehydrators permanently installed in R-12 systems for naval ships are designed to remove only the minute quantities of moisture unavoidably introduced into the system. Extreme care must be taken to prevent moisture, or moisture-laden air, from entering the system.

G. Cleaning The System

Systems may accumulate dirt and scale as a result of improper techniques used during repair or installation. If such dirt is excessive and a tank-type cleaner is available, connect the cleaner to the compressor suction strainer. Where such a cleaner is not available, a hard wool felt filter, about 5/16 inch thick, should be inserted in the suction strainer screen. The plant should be operated with an operator in attendance, for at least 36 hours or until cleaned, depending upon the size and condition of the plant.

IV. DETECTING AND CORRECTING TROUBLES

Faulty operation of the refrigerating plant is indicated by various definite symptoms. These symptoms may indicate the presence of one or more conditions in the plant. Each condition must be eliminated by specific corrective measures. Space does not permit a detailed discussion here of abnormal plant conditions, but you can find complete information in the manufacturer's technical manual furnished with each refrigeration plant.

The following chart, listing symptoms, their causes, and the corrective measures to be taken, will assist you in correcting faulty operation quickly and efficiently.

| A. Trouble-Diagnosis Chart |||
|---|---|---|
| Symptom or difficulty | Condition may be due to | Correction |
| High suction pressure | Overfeeding of expansion valve | Regulate expansion valve, check thermal element attachment. |
| | Leaky suction valves | Examine valve disks, or piston rings; replace if defective. |
| | Improper functioning of low-pressure control switch Discharge valves leak slightly | Readjust or replace switch. Examine valves. If leaking, replace if necessary. |
| Low suction pressure | Restricted liquid line, expansion valve, or suction strainers | Remove, examine, and clean strainers. |
| | Insufficient refrigerant in system | Check for refrigerant shortage. |
| | Too much oil circulating in system | Check for too much oil in circulation. Remove oil. (See "Oil leaves crank-case.") Adjust valve to give more flow. |
| | Improper adjustment of expansion valves | |
| | Coils in refrigerators clogged with frost | Defrost coils. |
| | Thermal bulb of expansion valve has lost charge | Detach thermal bulb from suction line and hold in the palm of one hand, with the other hand gripping the suction line; if flooding through is observed, bulb has not lost its charge. If no flooding through is noticed, test and replace expansion valve if necessary. |
| | Forced air cooler airflow restricted or fan inoperative One or more solenoid valves closed Compressor capacity in excess of existing compartment heat load | Check for air obstruction, dirty filters, or faulty electrical operation. Check electrical solenoid circuit for failure, and repair. Reduce speed of compressor or adjust compressor capacity reduction where provided. |
| Low suction line temperature | Excessive liquid refrigerant circulating in system | Check expansion valve adjustment and regulate. |
| High suction line temperature | Shortage of refrigerant in system | Check, test for leaks and add refrigerant as required. |

## Trouble-Diagnosis Chart — Continued

| Symptom or difficulty | Condition may be due to | Correction |
|---|---|---|
| High discharge pressure | Air or noncondensable gas in system Inlet water warm No water or insufficient quantity of water flowing through condenser Condenser tubes clogged Too much refrigerant in system (condenser tubes submerged in liquid refrigerant) Condenser improperly vented Air-cooled condenser dirty or receiving insufficient air | Purge air from condenser. Increase quantity by adjusting water-regulating valve. Adjust water-regulating valve, open manual valves, or start pump. Clean condenser tubes and water boxes. Draw off excess refrigerant into service drum. Vent condenser water boxes. Clean or remove obstructions. Check space ventilation for adequate supply of cool air and correct. |
| Low discharge pressure | Too much water flowing through condenser Water too cold or unthrottled Liquid refrigerant flooding back from cooling coils Leaky discharge valve | Regulate water valve. Reduce quantity of water. Change expansion valve adjustment, examine fastening thermal element. Examine. If leaking, replace. |
| High discharge temperature | Air or noncondensable gas in system | Purge air from condenser. |

## Trouble-Diagnosis Chart — Continued

| Symptom or difficulty | Condition may be due to | Correction |
|---|---|---|
| Low discharge temperature | Excessive liquid refrigerant in system | Check expansion valve setting and adjust. |
| Low oil pressure | Dirt in oil pump or strainer | Stop compressor. Check oil gage for accuracy. Clean, repair, or replace oil strainer and pump. |
| Excessive oil pressure | Clogged oil distribution lines | Stop compressor. Check oil gage for accuracy. Pump down, clean oil lines. |
| Oil leaves crankcase | Refrigerant flooding back to compressor Leaking piston rings or worn cylinder Expansion valves leaking Overcharge of oil | Adjust expansion valve and check for proper mounting of thermal elements. Replace rings, cylinder sleeves, or compressor. Rebore and refit. Valve seats and stem may be corroded from passage of refrigerant vapor. Check and replace if required. Check oil sight glass and remove excess. Check for continuing return and repeat process until oil level is constant. |
| Oil does not return to crankcase | Expansion valve not supplying cooling coil with sufficient refrigerant Valve in oil return line closed or stuck shut Oil trap or pocket in cooling coil or suction line piping | Check operation of expansion valve and adjust, if required. Open. Locate, open, and drain. |
| Oil sight glass shows presence of oil foaming | Excessive liquid refrigerant returning to compressor | Check expansion valve adjustment or leaking hand expansion valves. Adjust, repair, or replace. |
| Crankcase and cylinder temperature relatively warm with low suction pressure | Shortage of refrigerant | Test for shortage, add refrigerant if required, test for leaks. |
| Crankcase temperature relatively cooler than suction line with low pressure suction | Excessive oil is circulating in system | See "Oil leaves crankcase." |
| Crankcase and cylinder temperature relatively cold, sweating, or frosting | Liquid refrigerant being returned to compressor | Check expansion valve setting, adjust. Check for proper mounting of thermal element. |
| Compressor noisy | Vibration because the compressor is not rigidly | Bolt down rigidly. |

## Trouble-Diagnosis Chart — Continued

| Symptom or difficulty | Condition may be due to | Correction |
|---|---|---|
| Compressor noisy— (Continued) | bolted to foundation Too much oil in circulation causing hydraulic knock Slugging due to flooding back of refrigerant Wear of parts such as piston pins, bearings, etc. | Check oil level. Expansion valve open too wide; adjust. Thermo-bulb incorrectly placed or loose; check and relocate or fasten. Determine location of cause. Repair compressor. |
| Water supply pressure too low | Water pump suction line restricted Pressure-reducing valve in fire flushing line improperly adjusted | Check for closed valves, check strainer and clean. Check and readjust. |
| Water supply pressure too high | Pressure-reducing valve improperly adjusted Water valves open too wide. | Check and adjust. Check and close to proper pressure. |
| Water overboard temperature too low | Excessive water flow through condenser | Correlate with discharge pressure and check water regulating valve operation, adjust if necessary. (See "Water supply pressure too high.") |
| Water overboard temperature too high | Restricted water flow through condenser | Correlate with discharge pressure. Check water-regulating valve and adjust, if necessary. (See "Water supply pressure too low.") |
| Liquid line refrigerant temperature too warm | High condensing temperature | Check condenser for water quantity. |
| Liquid line refrigerant temperature too cold | Shortage of refrigerant Excessive oil in circulation | Test for shortage, charge with refrigerant, test for R-12 leakage. See "Oil leaves crankcase." |
| Sight flow indicator shows bubbles in refrigerant | Shortage of refrigerant | Test for shortage, charge with refrigerant, test for R-12 leakage. |
| Ice-making tank temperature too high | Automatic controls not functioning Brine solution too weak and freezing | Check electrical circuit for open switches, blown fuses, burnt solenoid coil, and repair or replace. Check adjustment of control switch. Check salinity of brine for proper density. Add stronger solution. |

## Trouble-Diagnosis Chart Continued

| Symptom or difficulty | Condition may be due to | Correction |
|---|---|---|
| Ice-making tank temperature too high (Continued) | Expansion valve not feeding sufficient refrigerant | Check for improper adjustment, or moisture at valve orifice. Adjust or clean. Put dehydrator in operation if moisture is in evidence. |
| Ice-making tank temperature too low | Automatic controls not functioning Hand expansion valve leaking | Check solenoid valve switch setting and adjust if necessary. Check position of valve for tight closing. Check for dirt or corrosion at seat and pin. Clean, repair, or replace. |
| Compartment temperature too high | Automatic controls not functioning Excessive frost on cooling coils Expansion valve not feeding sufficient refrigerant Airflow restricted on forced air coolers Excessive infiltration of uncooled air | Check solenoid valve switch or thermostat setting, electrical circuit, fuses, and solenoid coil. Repair or replace. If there is a forced air cooler, check to see that fan is operating. Defrost. Check for improper adjustment, or moisture at valve orifice. Adjust or clean. Put dehydrator in operation if moisture is present. Check filters, duct work obstructions, and fan operation. Clean and repair as required. Check unwarranted traffic in and out of compartment. Take steps to limit traffic as to personnel and entrance periods. Check compartment openings and door gaskets. Repair or replace. |
| | Introduction of warm and/ or moist product | Temporary. If within the capacity of equipment, temperature will eventually return to normal. Start an additional compressor if system is arranged for isolating loads carried by more than one unit in operation. |

| | | |
|---|---|---|
| Compartment temperature too low | Automatic controls not functioning<br>Hand expansion valve leaking | Check solenoid valve switch or thermostat setting, electrical circuit, fuses, and solenoid coils. Repair or replace. Check position of valve for tight closing. Check for dirt, or corrosion at seat and pin. Clean, repair, or replace. |
| Liquid refrigerant cycling through the cooling coil with wide variation in superheat at thermal element location | Excessive oil circulating through system<br>Moisture or ice at thermal element contact with | Check other symptoms for a like condition. (See "Oil leaves crankcase" and "Oil does not return to crankcase.") Remove, dry, and properly insulate. |

## Trouble-Diagnosis Chart Continued

| Symptom or difficulty | Condition may be due to | Correction |
|---|---|---|
| Liquid refrigerant cycling through the cooling coil with wide variation in superheat at thermal element location (Continued) | suction line affecting true operation Expansion valve defective Thermal element located in such a position as to be affected by airflow Expansion valve too large or has improper thermo-static charge Moisture in expansion valve port or working parts | Check thermal element for response. Repair or replace. Remove and relocate; insulate. See technical manual furnished with equipment for selected size and type. Install proper valve. Check heat valve body slowly taking care not to damage power element and gaskets. Heat will temporarily free valve parts and resume automatic operation. If moisture is present disassemble valve, clean and replace. Put dehy-drator into service. |
| Liquid refrigerant carrying through the coil and far beyond the thermal element location with little superheat at this point | Expansion valve open too wide Thermal element making poor contact with suction piping Thermal element improperly located or insulated. Expansion valve leaking | Adjust to close. Remove, clean both surfaces, and insulate. Remove, locate properly, and insulate. When compressor shuts down, check by listening at valve for a hissing sound. Check for dirt or corrosion of seat. Clean, repair, or replace. |
| Liquid refrigerant carrying partially through the coil with considerable superheat at thermal element location | Moisture in expansion valve port or working parts Liquid line strainer clogged or dirty Expansion valve improperly adjusted Shortage of refrigerant Expansion valve thermal element improperly located Expansion valve too small Refrigerant gas in liquid line | See same condition and correction as above. Remove, clean, and replace. Check superheat and adjust. Check storage, test for leaks and charge. Check and relocate. See technical manual furnished with equipment, and install proper size and type. Check for excessive pressure loss in liquid line. Open valves or restrictions affecting loss. Check subcooler, if installed, for proper operation. |

| Trouble-Diagnosis Chart Continued | | |
|---|---|---|
| Symptom or difficulty | Condition may be due to | Correction |
| Liquid refrigerant carrying partially through the coil with considerable superheat at thermal element location- (Continued) | Pressure drop through cooling coils excessive Expansion valve power element has lost charge of refrigerant Expansion valve equalizer line closed or restricted Expansion valve thermal element being affected by refrigerant from another cooling coil circuit | Check for restrictions, oil traps or valves partially closed. Drain oil or open restrictions as applicable. Remove thermal element and hand-warm to body temperature. If not responsive, replace power assembly or valve. Check, and open or replace.<br>Check location of thermal element. Remove and properly locate. |
| Compressor will not start | Overload tripped, fuses blown Switch out No charge of gas in system operated by low-pressure control switch Solenoid valves closed No flow of circulating water through condenser to actuate water-failure switch | Reset overload, replace fuses, and examine for cause of condition. Throw in switch. With no gas in system there is insufficient pressure to throw in low-pressure control. Recharge system with refrigerant; check and repair leaks. Examine coil, switch, etc.; if defective or out of adjustment, replace or adjust. Provide condenser circulating water. |
| Compressor runs continuously | Shortage of refrigerant Discharge or suction valves leak badly Head gasket blown between cylinders Improper functioning of low-pressure control switch Overloaded compressor Stuck-open or leaky relief valve | Test for shortage of refrigerant; if insufficient, add proper amount. Test system for leaks.<br>Test valves; if leaking, repair or replace. Replace gasket. Adjust or replace switch. Start an additional compressor if system is arranged for isolating loads carried by more than one unit in operation. Overhaul relief valve. |
| Compressor short cycles on high pressure cutout | High pressure cutout incorrectly set. | Check setting of high pressure cutout; switch should throw out at about 150 pounds head pressure. |

| Trouble-Diagnosis Chart Continued | | |
|---|---|---|
| Symptom or difficulty | Condition may be due to | Correction |
| Compressor short cycles on low-pressure control switch | Low-pressure control incorrectly set. (See "Low suction pressure.") | Check setting and adjust. |
| Water valve chatters | Water pressure too high | Reduce water pressure by adjusting water pressure-reducing valve or throttling stop valve. |
| Water runs continuously when compressor *is* shut off | Water-regulating valve open too wide<br>Dirt under seat of water-regulating valve<br>Valve mechanism stuck<br>Pump motor controller contact stuck shut | Readjust valve to give correct head pressures corresponding to water inlet temperature and condensing pressure. Remove valve from lines, disassemble, and examine; replace defective parts, clean and reassemble. If valve then does not function properly, replace. Remove and disassemble. Clean valve seats and valve pins, lubricate, adjust packing, etc. Adjust |
| Head gasket leaks | Head bolts stretched, or washers crushed Oil or refrigerant slugging | Examine gaskets; replace if necessary. Tighten head bolts. Replace washers. Check operating conditions for flooding of refrigerant back to compressor. Correct. |
| Oil seepage at shaft seal connection is excessive | Failure of shaft seal | Test, repair, or replace crankshaft seal. |
| Oil seepage at refrigerant system piping and compressor connections | Leakage of refrigerant | Test; remake connections or provide replacement gaskets, as required. |

# GLOSSARY OF ENGINEERING TERMS

## TABLE OF CONTENTS

| | Page |
|---|---|
| Automatic Bus Transfer ... Boiler Tube Cleaner | 1 |
| Boiler Water ... Distillate | 2 |
| Distilling Plants ... Forging | 3 |
| Fresh Water System ... Log Book | 4 |
| Log, Engineering ... Parts Per Million | 5 |
| Preheating ... Static | 6 |
| Steam Lance ... Wireways | 7 |
| Work Request ... Zinc | 8 |

# GLOSSARY OF ENGINEERING TERMS

ABT (AUTOMATIC BUS TRANSFER): An automatic electrical device that supplies power to vital equipment. This device will shift from the normal power supply to an alternate power supply when the normal supply is interrupted.

ACETYLENE: A gas that is chemically produced from calcium carbide and water, used for welding and cutting.

ADAPTER: A coupling or similar device that permits fittings with different-sized openings (apertures) to be joined together.

AIR EJECTOR: A type of jet pump, used to remove air and other gases from the condensers.

AIR CHAMBER: A chamber, usually bulb-shaped, on the suction and discharge sides of a pump. Air in the chamber acts as a cushon and prevents sudden shocks to the pump.

AIR REGISTER: A device in the casing of a boiler, used for regulating the amount of air for combustion and to provide a circular motion to the air.

AISE: Association of Iron and Steel Engineers.

ALLOY: A mixture composed of two or more metals.

ALTERNATING CURRENT (A-C): Current that is constantly changing in value and direction at regular recurring intervals.

AMBIENT TEMPERATURE: The temperature of the surrounding area.

AMMETER: An instrument for measuring the rate of flow of electrical current in amperes.

ANNEALING: The softening of metal by heating and slow cooling.

ANNUNCIATOR: See ENGINE ORDER TELEGRAPH.

ARGON: An inert gas, slightly heavier than air, used in inert-gas shielded metal arc welding.

ARMORED CABLE: An electric cable that is protected on the outside by a metal covering.

ASTM: American Society for Testing Metals.

AUTOMATIC COMBUSTION CONTROL SYSTEM (ACC): A system that provides a means of automatically controlling the fuel and air mixture in a boiler.

BACK PRESSURE: The pressure exerted on the exhaust side of a pump or engine.

BDC (BOTTOM DEAD CENTER): The position of a reciprocating piston at its lowest point of travel.

BALLASTING: The process of filling empty tanks with salt water, to protect the ship from underwater damage and increase its stability. See DEBALLASTING.

BLUEPRINTS: Reproduced copies of drawings (usually having white lines on a blue background.

BOILER: A strong' metal tank or vessel composed of tubes, drums, and headers, in which water is heated by the gases of combustion to form steam.

BOILER CENTRAL CONTROL STATION: A centrally located station for directing the control of all boilers in the fireroom.

BOILER DESIGN PRESSURE: Pressure specified by the manufacturer, usually about 103% of normal steam drum operating pressure.

BOILER INTERNAL FITTINGS: All parts inside the boiler which control the flow of steam and water.

BOILER OPERATING PRESSURE: The pressure required to be maintained in a boiler while in service.

BOILER OPERATING STATION: A location from which boilers are operated.

BOILER RECORD SHEET: A NavShips form maintained for each boiler, which serves as a monthly summary of operation.

BOILER REFRACTORIES: Materials used in the boiler furnace to protect the boiler from heat of combustion.

BOILER ROOM: A compartment containing boilers but not containing a station for operating or firing the boilers. Refers specifically to bulkhead enclosed boiler installations.

BOILER TUBE CLEANER: A CYLINDRICAL brush that is used to clean the insides of boiler tubes.

BOILER WATER: Refers to the water actually contained in the boiler.

BRAZING: A method of joining two metals at high temperature with a molten alloy.

BRINE: A highly concentrated solution of salt in water, normally associated with the overboard discharge of distilling plants.

BRITTLENESS: That property of a material which causes it to fracture prior to any noticeable signs of deformation.

BURNERMAN: Man in fireroom who tends the burners in the boilers.

BUSHING: A renewable lining for a hole through which a moving part passes.

BYPASS: To divert the flow of gas or liquid. Also, the line that diverts the flow.

CALIBRATION: The comparison of any measuring instrument with a set standard.

CANTILEVER: A projecting arm or beam supported only at one end.

CAPILLARY TUBE: A slender thin-walled small-bored tube used with remote-reading indicators.

CARBON DIOXIDE: A colorless, orderless gas used as a fire extinguishing agent and for inflating liferafts and lifejackets.

CARBON PACKING: Pressed segments of graphite used to prevent steam leakage around shafts.

CASUALTY POWER SYSTEM: A means of using portable cables to transmit power to vital equipment in an emergency.

CHECK VALVE: A valve that permits a flow of liquid in one direction only.

CHILL SHOCKING: A method of removing scale from the tubes of a distilling plant, utilizing steam and cold water.

CHLORINE: A heavy gas, greenish-yellow in color used for water purification, sewage disposal, and in the preparation of bleaching solutions. Poisonous in concentrated form.

CIRCUIT BREAKER: An electrical device that provides circuit overload protection.

CLUTCH: A form of coupling which is designed to connect or disconnect a driving or driven member.

COMPARTMENT CHECKOFF LIST: A list of all damage control fittings, their location, and status for different ship conditions.

CONDENSER: A heat transfer device in which steam or vapor is condensed to water.

CONDUCTION: A method of heat transfer from one body to another when the two bodies are in physical contact.

CONSTANT PRESSURE GOVERNOR: A device that maintains a constant pump discharge pressure under varying loads.

CONTROLLER: A device used to stop, start, and protect motors from overloads, while they are running.

CORROSION: The process of being eaten away gradually by chemical action, such as rusting.

COUNTERSINK: A cone-shaped tool used to enlarge and bevel one end of a drilled hole.

CROSS-CONNECTED PLANT: A method of operating two or more plants as one unit, having a common steam supply.

CURTIS STAGE: A velocity-compounded impulse turbine stage having one pressure drop in the nozzles and two velocity drops in the blading.

DEAERATING FEED TANK (DA TANK): A unit in the steam-water cycle used to (1) free the condensate of dissolved oxygen, (2) heat the feed water, and (3) act as a reservoir for feed water.

DEBALLASTING: The process of emptying salt from tanks, to protect the ship from underwater damage and increase its stability.

DEGREE OF SUPERHEAT: The amount by which the temperature of steam exceeds saturation temperature.

DIATOMACEOUS EARTH: A light, crumbly silica material derived from algae and microscopic skeletons. It has relatively high absorption and filtering qualities.

DIATOMITE FILTERS: Filters made of a diatomaceous earth and asbestos filler.

DIRECT CURRENT (D-C): Current that moves in one direction only.

DIRECT DRIVE: One in which the drive mechanism is coupled directly to the driven member.

DISTILLATE: Fresh water produced in distilling plants.

DISTILLING PLANTS: Units commonly called evaporators (evaps) used to convert seawater into fresh water.

DRAWING: The plans used to show the fabrication and assembly details.

DRUM, STEAM: The large tank at the top of the boiler in which the steam collects.

DRUM, WATER: A tank at the bottom of a boiler; also called MUD DRUM.

DRY PIPE: A perforated pipe at the highest point in a steam drum to collect steam.

DUCTILITY: Property possessed by metals that allows them to be drawn or stretched.

ECONOMIZER: A heat transfer device on a boiler that uses the gases of combustion to preheat the feed water.

EDUCTOR: A jet type pump (no moving parts) used to empty flooded spaces.

EFFICIENCY: The ratio of the output to the input.

ELASTICITY: The ability of a material to return to its original size and shape.

ELECTRODE: A metallic rod (welding rod) used in electric welding that melts when current is passed through it.

ELECTROHYDRAULIC STEERING: A system having a motor-driven hydraulic pump that creates the force needed to actuate the rams to position the ship's rudder.

ELECTROLYSIS: A chemical action that takes place between unlike metals in systems using salt water.

ELECTROMOTIVE FORCE (EMF): A force that causes electrons to move through a closed circuit; expressed in volts.

ELEMENT: A substance which consists of chemically united atoms of one kind.

ENERGY: The capacity for doing work.

ENGINEER'S BELL BOOK: A legal record maintained by the throttle watch of all ordered main engine speed changes.

ENGINE ORDER TELEGRAPH: A device on the ship's bridge to give orders to the engine-room. Also called ANNUNCIATOR.

EPM (EQUIVALENTS PER MILLION): The number of equivalent parts of a substance per million parts of another substance. The word "equivalent" refers to the equivalent weight of a substance.

EXPANSION JOINT: A junction which allows for expansion and contraction.

FATIGUE: The tendency of a material to break under repeated strain.

FEED HEATER: A heat transfer device used to heat the feed water before it goes to the boiler.

FEED WATER: Fresh water, with the highest possible level of purity, made in EVAPORATORS for use in boilers.

FERROUS METAL: Metal with a high iron content.

FIREBOX: The section of a ship's boiler where fuel oil combustion takes place.

FIREMAIN: The salt water line that provides fire-fighting and flushing water throughout the ship.

FIRE TUBE BOILER: Boilers in which the gases of combustion pass through the tubes and heat the water surrounding them.

FLAREBACK: A backfire of flame and hot gases into a ship's fireroom from the firebox. Caused by a fuel oil explosion in the firebox.

FLASH POINT OF OIL: That temperature at which the oil vapor will flash into fire but the main body of the oil will not ignite.

FLEXIBLE I-BEAM: An I-shaped steel beam on which the forward end of a turbine is mounted; it allows for longitudinal expansion and contraction.

FLOOR PLATES: The removable deck plating of a fireroom or engineroom aboard ship.

FLUX: A chemical agent that retards oxidation of the surface, removes oxides already present, and aids fusion.

FORCE: Anything that tends to produce or modify motion.

FORCED DRAFT: A term used to describe air under pressure supplied to the burners in a ship's boiler.

FORCED DRAFT BLOWERS: Turbine-driven fans which supply air to the boiler furnace.

FORCED FEED LUBRICATION: A lubrication system that uses a pump to maintain a constant pressure.

FORGING: The forming of metal by heating and hammering.

FRESH WATER SYSTEM: A piping system which supplies fresh water throughout the ship.

FUEL OIL MICROMETER VALVE: A valve installed at the burner manifold, which is used to control the fuel oil pressure to the burners.

FUEL OIL SERVICE TANKS: Tanks from which the fuel oil service pumps take suction for discharging oil to the burners.

FUSE: A protective device that is designed to open a circuit if the current flow exceeds a predetermined value.

GAGE GLASS: A device for indicating the liquid level in a tank.

GAS-FREE: A term used to describe a space that has been tested and found safe for hot work (welding & cutting).

GEARED-TURBINE DRIVE: A turbine that drives a pump, generator, or other machinery through reduction gears.

GROUNDED PLUG: A three pronged electrical plug used for grounding portable tools to the ship's structure. It is a safety device which always must be checked prior to using portable tools.

HAGEVAP SOLUTION: A chemical compound used in distilling plants, to prevent the formation of scale.

HALIDE LEAK DETECTOR: A device that is used to locate leaks in refrigeration systems.

HANDHOLE: An opening that is large enough for the hand and arm to enter the boiler for making slight repairs, and for inspection.

HANDY BILLY: A small portable water pump.

HARDENING: The heating and rapid cooling (quenching) of metal to induce hardness.

HARDNESS: The ability of a material to resist penetration.

HEAT EXCHANGER: Any device that is designed to allow the transfer of heat from one fluid (liquid or gas) to another.

HYDROGEN: A highly explosive, light, invisible, non-poisonous gas used for underwater welding and cutting operations.

HYDROMETER: An instrument used for determining the specific gravity of liquids.

HYDROSTATIC TEST: A pressure test using water to detect leaks in a boiler or other closed systems.

IGNITION, COMPRESSION: Ignition where the heat generated by compression in an internal combustion engine ignites the fuel (as in a diesel engine).

IGNITION, SPARK: Ignition where the mixture of air and fuel in an internal combustion-engine is ignited by an electric spark (as in a gasoline engine).

IMPELLER: An encased, rotating element provided with vanes which draw in fluid at the center and expel it at a high velocity at the outer edge.

IMPULSE TURBINE: A turbine in which the major part of the driving force is received from the impulse of incoming steam.

INDIRECT DRIVE: A drive mechanism coupled to the driven member by gears or belts.

INERT: Inactive.

INJECTOR: A device which, by means of a jet of steam, forces water into the boiler, or as in the diesel engineforces fuel into the cylinders.

INSULATION: A material used to retard heat transfer.

JACKBOX: Receptacle, usually secured to a bulkhead, in which telephone jacks are mounted.

JOB ORDER: The order issued by a repair activity to its own subdivisions, to perform a repair job in response to a WORK REQUEST.

JUMPER: Any connecting pipe, hose, or wire, normally for use in emergencies aboard ship, used to bypass damaged sections of a pipe, a hose, or & wire. (See BYPASS.)

JURY RIG: Any temporary or makeshift device.

LABYRINTH PACKING: Rows of metallic strips or fins used to prevent steam leakage along the shaft or a turbine.

LAGGING: A protective and confining cover placed over insulating material.

LIGHT OFF: Start, literally; 'to start a fire in," as in "light off a boiler."

LOG BOOK: Any chronological record of events, such as an engineering watch log.

LOG, ENGINEERING: A legal record of important events and data concerning the machinery of a ship.

LOG ROOM: Engineer's office on board ship.

LUBE OIL PURIFIER: A unit that removes water and sediment from lubricating oil by centrifugal force.

MACHINABILITY: The term used to describe the ease with which a metal may be turned, planed, milled, or otherwise shaped.

MAIN CONDENSER: A heat exchanger which converts exhaust steam to feed water.

MAIN DRAIN SYSTEM: The system used for pumping bilges, consisting of pumps and associated piping.

MAKEUP FEED: Water of required purity intended for use in ship's boilers. It is the water needed to replace that lost in the steam cycle.

MALLEABILITY: That property of a material which enables it to be stamped, hammered, or rolled into thin sheets.

MANIFOLD: A fitting with numerous branches used to convey fluids between a large pipe and several smaller pipes.

MECHANICAL ADVANTAGE (MA): The advantage (leverage) gained by the use of such devices as a wheel to open a large valve, chain falls and block and tackle to lift heavy weights, and wrenches to tighten nuts on bolts.

MECHANICAL CLEANING: A method of cleaning the firesides of boilers by scraping and wire-brushing.

MICROMHOS: Electrical units used with salinity indicators for measuring the conductivity of water.

MOTOR GENERATOR SET: A machine which consists of a motor mechanically coupled to a generator and usually mounted on the same base.

NAVY BOILER COMPOUND: A powdered chemical mixture used in boiler water treatment to convert scale-forming salts into sludge.

NAVY SPECIAL FUEL OIL (NSFO): The name applied to the grade of fuel oil that the Navy uses in combatant ships.

NIGHT ORDER BOOK: A notebook containing standing and special instructions by the engineer officer to the night engineering officer of the watch.

NITROGEN: An inert gas which will not support life or combustion. Used in recoil systems and other spaces requiring an inert atmosphere.

NONFERROUS METAL: Metals that are composed primarily of some element or elements other than iron.

OFFICER OF THE WATCH (OOW): Officer on duty in the engineering spaces.

OIL KING: A petty officer who receives, transfers, discharges, and tests fuel oil and maintains fuel oil records.

OIL POLLUTION ACTS: The Oil Pollution Act of 1924 (as amended) and the Oil Pollution Act of 1961 prohibit the overboard discharge of oil and water containing oil in port, in any sea area within 50 miles of land, and in special prohibited zones.

ORIFICE: A small opening.

OVERLOAD RELAY: An electrical protective device which automatically trips when a circuit draws excessive current.

OXIDATION: The process of various elements and compounds combining with oxygen. The corrosion of metals is generally a form of oxidation; rust on iron, for example, is iron oxide or oxidation.

PANT, PANTING: A series of pulsations caused by minor, recurrent explosions in the firebox of a ship's boiler. Usually caused by a shortage of air.

PERIPHERY: The curved line which forms the boundary of a circle (circumference), ellipse, or similar figure.

PITOMETER LOG: Device for indicating speed of ship and distance traveled by measuring water pressure on a tube projected outside the ship's hull.

PLASTICITY: That property which enables a material to be excessively and permanently deformed without breaking.

PNEUMERCATOR: A type of manometer used for measuring the volume of liquid in tanks.

PPM (PARTS PER MILLION): A comparison of the number of parts of a substance in a million parts of another substance. Used to measure the salt content of water.

PREHEATING: The application of heat to the base metal prior to a welding or cutting operation.

PRIME MOVER: The source of motion as a turbine, automobile engine, etc.

PUNCHING TUBES: The name applied to the mechanical means of cleaning the interiors of boiler tubes.

RADIATION, HEAT: The process of emitting heat in the form of heat waves.

REACH RODS: A length of pipe or back stock used as an extension on valve stems.

REACTION TURBINE: A turbine in which the major part of the driving force is received from the reactive force of steam leaving the blading.

REDUCER: Any coupling or fitting which connects a large opening to a smaller pipe or hose.

REDUCING VALVES: Automatic valves which are used to provide a steady pressure lower than the supply pressure.

REDUCTION GEAR: A set of gears used to transmit the rotation of one shaft to another at a slower speed.

REEFER: A provision cargo ship or a refrigerated compartment. An authorized abbreviation for refrigerator.

REFRIGERANT 12 (R-12): A nonpoisonous gas that is used in air conditioning and refrigeration systems.

REGULATOR (GAS): An instrument used to control the flow of gases from compressed gas cylinders.

REMOTE OPERATING GEAR: Flexible cables attached to valve wheels which permit the valves to be operated from another compartment.

RISER: A vertical pipe leading off a larger one; e.g., fireman riser.

ROOT VALVE: A valve located where a branch line comes off the main line.

ROTARY SWITCH: An electrical switch which closes or opens the circuit by a rotating motion.

SAE: Society of Automotive Engineers.

SAFETY VALVES: An automatic, quick opening and closing valve which has a reseat-pressure lower than the lift pressure.

SALINOMETER: A hydrometer that measures the concentration of salt in a solution.

SATURATION PRESSURE: The pressure corresponding to the saturation temperature.

SATURATION TEMPERATURE: The temperature at which a liquid boils under a given pressure. For any given saturation temperature there is a corresponding saturation pressure.

SCALE: Undesirable deposit, mostly calcium sulfate, which forms in the tubes of boilers.

SENTINEL VALVES: Small relief valves used primarily as a warning device.

SHAFT ALLEY: The long compartment of a ship in which the propeller shafts revolve.

SKETCH: A rough drawing indicating major features of an object to be constructed.

SLIDING FEET: A mounting for turbines and boilers to allow for expansion and contraction.

SLUDGE: The sediment left in fuel oil tanks.

SOLID COUPLING: A device used to join two shafts rigidly.

SOOT BLOWER: A soot removal device using a steam jet to clean the firesides of a boiler.

SPECIFIC HEAT: The amount of heat required to raise the temperature of one gram of a substance $1^\circ C$. All substances are compared to water which has a specific heat of 1.

SPEED-LIMITING GOVERNOR: A device for limiting the rotational speed of a prime mover.

SPEED-REGULATING GOVERNOR: A device that maintains a constant speed on a piece of machinery that is operating under varying load conditions.

SPLIT PLANT: A method of operating propulsion plants so that they are divided into two or more separate and complete units.

SPRING BEARINGS: Bearings positioned at various intervals along a propulsion shaft to help keep it in alignment and support its weight.

SPRINKLING SYSTEM: An automatic watering system used for cooling and flooding magazines and cargo spaces in case of fire.

STATIC: A force exerted by reason of weight alone, related to bodies at rest or in balance.

STEAM LANCE: A device for using low pressure steam inside of boilers to remove soot and carbon from boiler tubes.

STEERING ENGINE: The machinery that turns the rudder.

STERN TUBE: A watertight enclosure for the propeller shaft.

STRAIN: The deformation or change in shape of a material resulting from the applied load.

STRENGTH: The ability of a material to resist strain.

STRESS: Force producing or tending to produce deformation of a metal.

STUFFING BOX: A device to prevent leakage between a moving and a fixed part in a steam engineering plant.

STUFFING TUBE: A packed tube making a watertight fitting through a bulkhead for a cable or small pipe.

SUMP: A container, compartment, or reservoir; used as a drain or receptacle for fluids.

SUPERHEATER: A unit in the boiler that drys the steam and raises its temperature.

SWASH PLATES: Metal plates in the lower part of the steam drum that prevent the surging of boiler water with the motion of the ship.

SWITCHBOARD: A panel or group of panels with automatic protective devices, used to distribute the electrical power throughout the ship.

TANK TOP: Top side of tank section or double bottom of a ship.

TDC (TOP DEAD CENTER): The position of a reciprocating piston at its uppermost point of travel.

TEMPERING: The heating and controlled cooling of a metal to produce the desired hardness.

THIEF SAMPLE: A sample of oil or water taken from a ship's tank for analysis.

THROTTLEMAN: Man in the engineroom who operates the throttles to control the main engines.

THRUST BEARING: A bearing designed to limit the end play and absorb the axial thrust of a shaft.

TO BLOW TUBES: A procedure, using steam, for removing soot and carbon from the tubes of steaming boilers.

TOP OFF: To fill up, as a ship tops off in fuel oil before leaving port.

TOUGHNESS: That property of a material which enables it to withstand shock, and to be deformed without breaking.

TRANSFORMER: An electrical device used to step up or step down an a-c voltage.

TRICK WHEEL: A steering wheel in the steering engineroom or emergency steering station of a ship.

TUBE EXPANDER: A tool used to expand replacement tubes into their seats in boiler drums and headers.

TURBINE: A multibladed rotor, driven by steam or hot gas.

TURBINE JACKING GEAR: A motor-driven gear arrangement used to slowly rotate idle propulsion shafts and turbines.

TURBINE STAGE: The term applied to one set of nozzles and the succeeding row or rows of moving blades.

UPTAKES (EXHAUST TRUNKS): Large enclosed passages for exhaust gases from boilers to the stacks.

VENT: A valve in a tank or compartment used primarily to permit air to escape.

VENTURI INJECTOR: A device used for washing the firesides of boilers.

VOID: A small empty compartment below decks.

VOLATILE: The term used to describe a liquid that vaporizes quickly.

VOLTAGE TESTER (WIGGINS): A portable instrument that is used to detect electricity.

WATER TUBE BOILER: Boilers in which the water flows through the tubes and is heated by the gases of combustion.

WATER WASHING: A method of cleaning the firesides of boilers to remove soot and carbon.

WELDING LEAD: The conductor through which the electrical current is transmitted from the power source to the electrode holder and welding rod.

WHELPS: Any of the ribs or ridges on the barrel of a capstan or windlass.

WIREWAYS: Passageways, between decks and on the overheads of compartments, that contain electric cables.

WORK REQUEST: Request issued to a naval shipyard, tender, or repair ship for repairs.

ZERK FITTING: A small fitting to which a grease gun can be applied to force lubricating grease into bearings or moving parts of machinery.

ZINC: A metal placed in salt water systems to counteract the effects of electrolysis.